DOWNSIZING DETROIT

DOWNSIZING DETROIT

The Future of the U.S. Automobile Industry

N. P. Kannan
Kathy K. Rebibo
Donna L. Ellis

Foreword by
Dr. John J. Fearnsides

Former Deputy Undersecretary and Chief Scientist
U.S. Department of Transportation

PRAEGER

PRAEGER SPECIAL STUDIES • PRAEGER SCIENTIFIC

Library of Congress Cataloging in Publication Data

Kannan, Narasimhan P.
 Downsizing Detroit.

 Bibliography: p.
 Includes index.
 1. Automobile industry and trade—United
States. I. Rebibo, Kathy K. II. Ellis, Donna L.
III. Title.
HD9710.U52K29 1982   338.4'76292'0973   82-11271
ISBN 0-03-060597-0

Published in 1982 by Praeger Publishers
CBS Educational and Professional Publishing
a Division of CBS Inc.
521 Fifth Avenue, New York, New York 10175 U.S.A.

© 1982   The MITRE Corporation

23456789 052 987654321

Printed in the United States of America

To

Charles A. Zraket

for his relentless efforts at improving public policies
through research and development

Foreword

The decline of the financial health of the U.S. automobile manufacturing industry is the most prominent example of this country's changing role in the world economy. The way in which the effects of this decline are managed or negotiated by business, labor, and government is likely to be indicative of the way in which the U.S. manages the transition from an industrially based economy to one based on services and high technology. This economic and social transition will not occur without pain. For many workers in automobile manufacturing, parts supply, and sales, there is unemployment and dislocation, a pattern that is repeated in other industries such as steel and textiles. For regional, state, and local governments there are the reduced financial bases and increased social costs that accrue as a result of a declining resident work force. For the nation as a whole, a suboptimal gross national product results as a consequence of the underutilization of its human resources.

When cast in economic terms, problems of unemployment and stagnant regional and national economies often seem abstract. They are not abstract, however, in human terms; indeed it has been said "statistics are people without tears." Media attention to the problems posed by high unemployment, a sluggish economy, high interest rates, and Administration cutbacks in domestic spending is increasing, as is the public's attention to the role that government, business, and labor officials should play to overcome these problems. This lack of agreement from these entities is likely to produce a long, painful, and not entirely successful transition to a knowledge-based rather than an industry based economy. Public reaction to continued economic stagnation is most forcefully expressed to the government; the electorate is unlikely to extend the terms of office of public officials who do not provide constructive solutions. No one is more aware of the political liabilities of high unemployment than those legislators running for reelection.

Successful management by government, business, and labor of the current economic transition will result only upon their recognition of the underlying nature of existing problems and their willingness to change the nature of long-established patterns of interrelating among themselves. The main problem facing the automobile industry is that the U.S. automobile manufacturing industry will probably never regain its previous share of the U.S. domestic market and is unlikely to dominate any emerging international markets. This means that even if sales increase with a resurgent economy, many of the million or so workers who have been furloughed in the past two years will not go back to their former jobs. This work force could diminish even further as industry invests in automation and/or as jobs are exported to take advantage of lower foreign wage rates.

One of the contributions of the work by Kannan, Rebibo, and Ellis is their acceptance of (and indeed insistence on) the fact of a permanently reduced market share for the U.S. automobile manufacturing industry. This enables them to begin exploring solutions as a complement to the growing and important literature describing what went wrong. That literature generally ascribes to U.S. labor costs some 25 percent of the estimated $1500 price difference between U.S. and Japanese cars of comparable size and quality. The remaining 75 percent is attributed to such management factors as inadequate quality control, low labor productivity, and inefficient management of parts, supplies, and inventory.

But a problem defined is not a problem solved. To expect U.S. labor to revert to prevailing wage rates in Japan and likely wage rates in such emerging industrial countries as Korea is to expect the abandonment of a quality of life not yet enjoyed by foreign workers. Moreover, the capital needed to increase the efficiency of production lines and associated inventory management procedures cannot be accrued immediately; nor are the effects of well-deployed capital assets instantaneous.[1] These conditions mean that U.S. manufacturers could be at a competitive disadvantage for a long time to come. They

---

1. For example, one of the many inventory control problems is the wide geographic dispersion of U.S. parts suppliers, which is more expensive and far less efficient than the Japanese "just-in-time" inventory management scheme. Bringing suppliers closer could also help in mitigating the economic depression in Detroit and other Midwest cities.

also mean that industry will consider the use of foreign labor and/or suppliers. In recognition of this fact, the Ford-United Automobile Workers (UAW) contract (and the recently approved UAW contract with General Motors) include wage and benefit concessions by the union in exchange for limitations on "outsourcing." These agreements also produced several innovative changes in the heretofore adversarial nature of labor-management relations, indicating a mutual awareness of the need to work together either to improve the industry's competitive position or at least to stem further erosion of its market share.

While industry and labor have begun to change many of their long-held positions, the executive and legislative branches of the U.S. federal government have responded as though restoration of the industry to its previous position of dominance were possible. The actions of two Administrations, while properly dealing with short-range problems, have not addressed the issue of permanent reductions in market share and, probably, total sales. For example, the Carter Administration's Chrysler Loan Guarantee Program, while providing temporary (and necessary) support for some Chrysler employees, may only be postponing the inevitable: a substantial corporate reorganization as required by bankruptcy laws, or a merger with a foreign manufacturer. The Reagan Administration, notwithstanding their emphasis on free market forces and, therefore, their disinclination to establish formal industrial policies, has negotiated a quota on imports of Japanese cars. Perhaps more importantly, the ability provided by last year's tax legislation for unprofitable companies to sell and lease back capital assets to get the benefits of tax credits is a clear policy of assisting troubled industries.[2] These initiatives are generally positive, interim responses to an obviously political and economic problem. They constitute a de facto (albeit short-term) U.S. industrial policy.

Given the pressures on members of Congress, it is impossible for the federal government not to have an industrial policy. The real question is whether that policy is clearly articulated and has specific long-range objectives or whether it is merely the net result of a series

---

2. Of course, there are those who argue that the new leasing rules — which are estimated to reduce federal revenues by some $27 billion by 1986 — were necessary to offset the advantages given profitable companies by the investment tax credit and accelerated cost recovery system provisions of the same tax law.

of expedient responses to political pressures. In this book, Kannan, Rebibo, and Ellis suggest specific solutions to the problems of easing the pains of transitioning to a less-dominant automobile manufacturing industry and preparing the nation's human resources for the service-oriented, high-technology future.

As to the latter, it is clear that a retraining program must be instituted to redirect now idle human resources to productive applications and to position the U.S. economy for the future. The goals of a retraining program must be consistent with some idea of the areas of increasing labor demand. This suggests that a long-range industrial policy — even if roughly formulated — is needed in addition to measures to provide financial assistance to the unemployed. Urgent action is needed, for example, to alleviate the current and estimated future shortages of engineers and skilled mechanics. The nation has adjusted in the past to sudden changes in required skill mixes; e.g., during the decline of the aerospace industry in the late 1960s and early 1970s. However, those adjustments have been difficult. Neither the people of Seattle, Washington nor the Boeing Company, for example, would like to see decline of the magnitude experienced before. But that experience produced some positive results. Indeed, as a result of considerable cooperation among industry, labor, and local government, Seattle now has a more diversified economy. Such cooperation is an essential element of any retraining or revitalization thrust. Federal financial assistance, while useful, could be counterproductive, especially if the conditions of assistance were based on poorly constructed (tacit or explicit) industrial policies.

In the long-term, it appears that the United States has a choice between investing in "reindustrialization," and ultimately accepting a work force that competes with and accepts the lower quality of life of workers in emerging industrialized countries, or investing in electronics, computers, biotechnology, and other emerging technologies — policies now being pursued by Japan, France, and the Federal Republic of Germany. Were it explained this way, it is difficult to perceive the U.S. public's not demanding an industrial policy from their political and industrial leadership.

Perhaps the reason that such a policy has not been forthcoming is the inability of government to implement such a policy in a way that is consistent with the national character and existing institutional structures. Much has been written about the government-business relationships in Japan and the Federal Republic of Germany. For an industrial policy to succeed in the U.S., however, it must be built on American attitudes, values, and institutions. Put more felicitously by Michael Maccoby in his new book, *The Leader*: "A successful leader draws out, promotes, and depends on attitudes and values that are shared by members of the group, class, or nation he leads. The leader's vision expresses goals in line with these values. . . . Leaders and those led differ in different cultures and historical periods." The lack of the average U.S. citizen's confidence in his government as expressed in many public opinion polls and by the widespread call for reduced taxes over the last several years seems to indicate that he will not accept approaches that rely heavily on central planning. This lack of confidence is even more pervasive in the business community. It may be, therefore, that while the federal government should lead the formulation of an industrial policy, its role in implementing such a policy should be less dominant.

In fact, as articulated by Kannan, Rebibo, and Ellis, as well as other commentators, the principal role in revitalizing the U.S. economy must be borne by U.S. management. Moreover, it is clear that if we are to remain competitive as a nation, some long-held management principles must be reevaluated and improved. Professor William Abernathy of the Harvard Business School — one of the most astute observers of the underlying problems of the U.S. automobile manufacturing industry — has pointed out the shortcomings of the general U.S. management trend toward maximizing short-term returns on investments (ROI).[3] It is now understood that this policy, ostensibly designed to respond to stockholders' interests in periods of high inflation, must be tempered by longer-range considerations if capital and labor are to be deployed in an optimal way. For example, such corporate strategies as diversification could have a much more positive public impact if acquisitions enhanced the opportunities for employees of existing corporate elements as well as increasing short-term ROI. In particular, diversification that provides a new business element that performs countercyclically to existing elements could materially increase opportunities for existing employees.

---

3. William J. Abernathy, Kim B. Clark, and Alan W. Kantrow. "The New Industrial Competition." *Harvard Business Review*. September/October 1981. Volume 59, Number 5. Boston, Mass.: Harvard University.

But does industry have a responsibility to its employees and to the public, which helps to bear the costs of unemployment? The answer seems to be "yes." The question is whether this responsibility can be accepted voluntarily by management as being in its own interest or whether new laws affecting corporate structure are needed. There is evidence that attention to labor's needs redound to the benefit of the corporation. The Japanese, for example, have demonstrated that the provision of "lifetime employment" positively impacts employee loyalty, morale, and productivity. Japanese firms are, however, much less dependent on their stockholders, relying more than their U.S. counterparts on debt, as opposed to equity, for capital formation. In addressing this issue, Kannan, Rebibo, and Ellis suggest an approach previously posited by Peter Drucker — the creation of corporate boards of directors that are independent of top management.[4] In this construct, professional managers who are able to devote considerable time to board activities would serve, say, nonrecurring five year terms on the board of directors. Thus, they would be able to devote ample time to the review of management performance but would not be affiliated with that corporation long enough to become protective of policies they helped to instigate. Such mechanisms, according to Drucker, would put teeth into the board's traditional functions of hiring and firing top management.

Actually, the Drucker concept embraces two board functions. The first as described above is the need for an executive committee to provide an independent review of top management performance on behalf of the stockholders. The second, which should be kept distinct from the first, is the need to communicate with the many constituencies any large business must deal with: banks, suppliers, labor, minority groups, local governments, and the general public. In an attempt to satisfy some of these, many corporations have added board members who represent particular constituencies. The problem, per Drucker, is that such members often represent their constituencies to the exclusion of more general corporate interests.

For example, one of the most important constituencies of any corporation is its labor base. New ways are obviously needed in the U.S. to restore employee loyalty and enthusiasm. It is likely that labor representation on the board, which was a condition of the

---

4. Peter F. Drucker, *Management: Tasks, Responsibilities, Practices.* New York: Harper & Row. 1974.

UAW agreement with Chrysler, is not the answer — at least in general. UAW representation on the boards of competing automobile manufacturers would constitute a clear conflict of interest. In this regard, the recent UAW agreements with Ford and General Motors established less formal consultative mechanisms. If in the process of developing a less adversarial relationship, U.S. management and labor develop individual, ad hoc mechanisms for increased consultation, it is unlikely that any federal action requiring labor representation on boards of directors would be deemed necessary.

Given the general laissez faire tendency of the U.S. as regards the social responsibility of large corporations, it is also unlikely that the federal government would impose requirements for board representation by, say, environmentalists. However, responsible social interaction with such entities is in the interest of the large corporation. It could forestall the imposition of mandatory as opposed to voluntary environmental standards.

As to the need for boards of directors that are independent of top management, it is clear that while the argument has considerable theoretical merit, it would likely cause a firestorm in Congress. Moreover, given the substantial increases in the level of international commercial competition, there is a greater incentive for U.S. businessmen than could be provided by government fiat. This is not to say, however, that government action would be inappropriate should management insist on maximizing their own interests at the expense of its human capital and the public at large.

In summary, it is in the interest of management, labor, and governments at all levels to work together to revitalize U.S. productivity to compete vigorously with emerging economic powers. This will require major attitudinal changes on the parts of all concerned. The role of government in achieving a new social contract is not clear. It is clear, however, that some explicit national industrial policy must be hammered out in cooperation with management and labor. This requires federal leadership, both in cooperatively developing an industrial policy and in articulating that policy to the public. It also requires improved management practices and a less adversarial labor/management relationship. It is time for coordinated action.

John J. Fearnsides
Director of Planning and Technology
The MITRE Corporation

Acknowledgments

We are grateful to the MITRE Corporation for supporting us with computer time and assisting in typing, editing, and graphics. MITRE'S support reflects their interest in the exposition of public policy research results and not their support for the views expressed in this book. Over the past two years we have also received valuable advice from Charles Zraket, William Gouse, Gordon MacDonald, Edward Sharp, Martin Scholl, Rodney Lay, Willard Fraize, Richard Manley, Pamela Walker, and Marc Kramer. We also benefited much from the numerous comments and advice of Dr. John Fearnsides, who also graciously agreed to write the foreword to this work. The meandering first draft of this book would not have seen print but for the diligent critique of Shirley True to whom we are deeply indebted.

We wish to thank Sharon Kosser, Laverna Lipp, Joyce Stellar, Lexie Kursteiner, Cheryl Cole, and Jody Jackson for their patient typing of numerous drafts; Jane Andrle for the graphics; Sharan Lieberman, Jill Hanna, and David Shumaker of the MITRE library for their valuable research assistance; and John McGowan for help on the index.

We wish to express our gratitude to Leslie Madden of the U.S. Department of Justice for her advice on environmental matters; Dan Bensing from the U.S Senate Staff for help on regulation; and Dave Power of J. D. Power and Associates for insights on consumer preferences. Dr. Donald Trilling, Executive Assistant to the Deputy Secretary, U.S. Department of Transportation; Cline Frasier of Draper Laboratory; Martin Anderson of the Future of the Automobile Program, Massachusetts Institute of Technology; Professor Lawrence White of New York University Business School; Professor William Abernathy of Harvard Business School; Maryann Keller of Paine Webber Mitchell Hutchins, Inc.; Paul Stersel of the Office of Highway Statistics, U.S. Department of Transportation; and Charles

Ardolini of the U.S. Department of Labor provided us with valuable information and advice for which we are extremely thankful.

We express our thanks to the representatives of General Motors Corporation, Ford Motor Company, and Chrysler Corporation who gave us the industry's viewpoints and information.

Finally, without the persistent encouragement from John Lambert of Praeger, this work would have taken twice as long to complete.

The authors assume full responsibility for any errors or omissions.

Contents

DOWNSIZING DETROIT

PART I
INTRODUCTION

1

Perspectives
on the Problem

The late Joseph Schumpeter characterized capitalism as a dynamic process of creative destruction in which new technologies and more efficient enterprises displace old ones.* As long as this process is gradual and involves only small businesses, it does not disrupt society. But when large, well-established corporations decline quickly, much hardship is inflicted on society in the form of loss of jobs. The adjustment problem gets even worse if the loss of jobs in one sector of the economy is not sufficiently offset by new opportunities elsewhere. In such adverse circumstances there is a justifiable need for government policies to ease the pain of transition. The U.S. automobile industry in its current depressed state is an excellent case in point.

THE LONG-TERM DECLINE

In this book we argue that the energy crises and the associated economic turmoil of the 1970s accelerated what would otherwise have been a gradual decline in the production of automobiles in the

---

*For an elaboration of this view see Schumpeter 1941, Ch. VII.

United States.* Currently there is an urgent need to help displaced workers from auto assembly plants and the related industries cope with the rapid change. This can be accomplished through a combination of short-term industry relief policies such as quotas, job training, regulatory reform, and so on. Some of these policies are already implemented. It is important, however, to realize that most government policies can help only in the next five to seven years as the long-term evolution of the industry is governed by a set of complex international economic and demographic forces that are outside the control of the U.S. government.

We postulate that domestic auto production will decline over the next two decades as other nations, particularly the developing ones, become increasingly industrialized. The auto industry's dilemma is a symptom of the general decline of the manufacturing sector of the U.S. economy, which has been slowly displaced by the service sector in recent decades. The current depression in the auto industry should be viewed more as a problem of rapid adjustment to structural changes in the market place than as a severe crisis that can be remedied by drastic government actions. In fact, any policies designed to "reindustrialize" or revive the domestic auto industry to its former dominant status are likely to fail. The reason is that such policies would be based on erroneous assumptions about the U.S. economy and its relationship with the rest of the world.

The United States is no longer an isolated economy as it was even three decades ago. U.S. trade with other nations, even the nonindustrialized countries, has increased by a factor of 18 since World War II. While it has gradually lost its long held advantage in manufactured goods to countries such as Japan, Taiwan, and Korea, it has emerged as a leader in high technology areas such as computers, communication, and professional services. Perhaps more significant, the United States has emerged as the leading exporter of sophisticated military weapons, largely as a result of Federal policies that have nurtured and protected our defense industry. Given this growing dependence of the United States on world trade, any actions on the part of government to insulate the

---

*It is important to note that the decline in U.S. auto production does not necessarily imply the decline of U.S. auto firms, which may continue to produce automobiles outside of the United States or merge with other international auto companies.

auto industry from international competition is likely to lead to a loss of jobs in our export sectors.

There are four major reasons for our long-term view. First, the U.S. industrial labor force has lost its monopoly in the world markets to the fast-growing skilled, but cheap, labor of the developing nations. Second, the automobile industry is highly coveted by most developing nations because of its material and labor intensive nature and for the beneficial economic multiplier effects. Third, the U.S. auto firms, which are emerging as multinational corporations with interests that are not necessarily consistent with the interests of the U.S. automobile workers, are increasingly becoming the active agents in the export of U.S. jobs to low-wage areas. Finally, the rapid worldwide rise in the price of petroleum in the past decade has effectively thwarted any growth in demand for automobiles in most developing nations. This leaves the U.S. market as one of the primary targets for automobile producers all over the world. We analyze each of these factors in the third chapter of this book.

THE SHORT-TERM TRANSITION

The best course of action for the nation is to accept the long-term decline of the U.S. auto production as inevitable, though not necessarily bad for the economy. It should be viewed as a part of the historical transition from a manufacturing to a service-oriented economy, which would have been stable and easier to cope with had it not been for the energy shocks and the consequent economic turmoil of the past decade. The current difficult transition calls for government policies to provide short-term help to the industry. Many policies have been proposed in public debates, ranging from job training, subsidies, and import quotas, to regulatory relief. In Chapters 4 through 7 we analyze each of these policies and conclude that both import quotas and sharp cuts in auto industry wages will help significantly, that there is very little justification for subsidies either to consumers or to the industry, and that there is an urgent need for reevaluating the entire basis for automobile-related regulations.

The principal recommendation to emerge from this work is that we need fundamental reforms in the institutional structure of the modern corporation, especially in the case of large, publicly held firms, to ensure that they are managed by competent professionals.

Otherwise these institutions can unwittingly jeopardize a substantial segment of our economy as in the case of the automobile industry. Recent studies suggest that the principal reason for the severity of the current crisis in the auto industry is poor management (Abernathy, Clark, and Kantrow 1981; Harbour 1981). An important area of reform is to make the corporate board of directors an independent body of full-time professionals. The board should truly represent the long-term stockholder interests by continuously monitoring the performance of the management, not only in terms of profitability, but also in terms of the intangibles such as consumer loyalty, employee morale, and long-term plans. This would lead to more efficient and well-managed enterprises and ensure that the larger interests of society are served.

The best way to understand the magnitude of damage a large industry can cause to the economy is to review the facts surrounding the recent crisis of the domestic automobile industry.

THE CURRENT SITUATION

The year 1980 was the worst in the history of the U.S. automobile industry. Together the big four domestic automakers — General Motors, Ford, Chrysler, and American Motors — liquidated over $4 billion or about 16 percent of their stockholders' equity. All four suffered severe losses (Table 1.1). General Motors, the world's largest manufacturer of automobiles, reported a loss for the first

TABLE 1.1
U.S. Automobile Manufacturers' Losses for 1980
(Million Dollars)

	Net Loss	Percent of Industry Losses	Percent of Industry Revenue
General Motors	763	18	54
Ford	1,543	37	35
Chrysler	1,710	41	9
American Motors	156	4	2
Total	4,172	100	100

Source: Standard and Poor's 1981b.

time since 1921. Chrysler, with only an 8.6 percent share of the industry's revenues, accounted for 41 percent of its losses. For Chrysler, 1980 was the third consecutive year of losses despite help from the U.S. government in the form of loan guarantees.* Ford Motor Company followed closely behind Chrysler with 37 percent of the industry's losses. Had it not been for the $0.5 billion profits from its overseas operations, Ford would have declared losses exceeding $2 billion, a record for a U.S. manufacturer. American Motors Corporation, the smallest of the four, with only a 2.5 percent share of the revenues, has since relinquished control to Renault, the French government-owned auto company.

A comparison of the auto industry after-tax rates of return with the rest of the domestic manufacturing industries revealed that, with the exception of Chrysler, the other automobile firms performed comparably well in 1978 and 1979. But in 1980, the rates of return for the auto industry plummeted to −9.5 percent, while for all of manufacturing it averaged 13.9 percent (Figure 1.1).

The plight of stockholders describes only part of the crisis faced by the auto industry. In addition to record losses, the industry laid off more than a quarter million workers or a third of the entire hourly workforce engaged in the production of automobiles (Table 1.2). Again, Chrysler Corporation fared the worst in terms of layoffs as a percent of the workforce. The peak unemployment rate for the industry reached a staggering 32 percent, worse than it was for the whole economy during the Great Depression. The unemployment rate in the auto industry was four times that of all manufacturing industries in the United States. In addition to jobs in auto manufacturing, an estimated 650 thousand jobs were lost in the support industries, primarily due to the closing of 99 supplier plants and 1650 domestic new car dealerships (U.S. Department of Transportation 1981a, p. 84).

As is well known, Detroit's dismal financial performance is the result of a sudden decline of sales of pasenger cars and light trucks,

---

*An agreement was signed between the U.S. government and the Chrysler Corporation in May 1980, which allowed loan guarantees of up to $1.5 billion under certain terms. Guarantees were made for $500 million in June 1980, $300 million in July 1980, and $400 million in January 1981. Major concessions were extracted in return from Chrysler's workers, creditors, and suppliers. (U.S. Congress, House, Committee on Banking, Finance and Urban Affairs 1981).

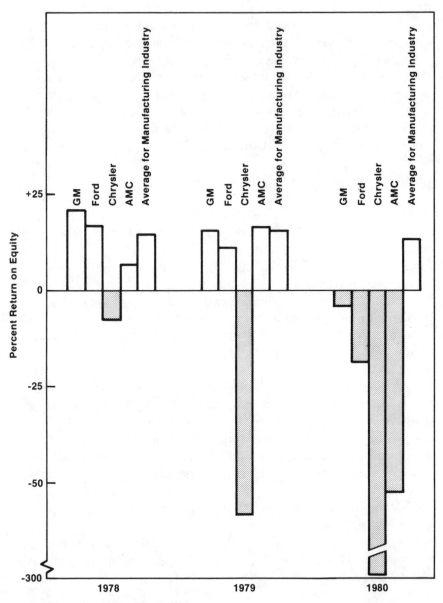

Source: Standard and Poor's 1981

Figure 1.1
After-Tax Return on Equity

TABLE 1.2
Auto Industry Peak Unemployment in 1980
(Thousand Workers)

	Total Hourly Workforce	Indefinite Layoffs	Percent of Workforce
General Motors	471	137.0	29
Ford	190	69.0	36
Chrysler	101	41.3	41
American Motors	16	2.7	17
Total	*778*	*250.0*	*32*

Source: U.S. Department of Transportation 1981, p. 85.

a decline due to a dramatic shift of consumer preferences toward smaller cars, particularly those built in Japan. In 1980, 64 percent of the new car market was captured by small cars (compacts, sub-compacts, and imports) compared to 56 percent in 1979 and 34 percent in 1971 (Figure 1.2). This shift in consumer preferences was caused by a set of unanticipated events, foremost of which was the Iranian crisis in late 1979 and the consequent rise in oil prices. Double-digit inflation rates, leading to very high interest rates, and the subsequent worldwide economic recession has further reduced the demand for cars.

While U.S. automakers faced a crisis situation, Japanese importers posted impressive gains in their share of the U.S. market. Japanese automobile exports to the United States rose from 11.5 percent in 1978 to 20 percent in 1980 (Figure 1.3). Moreover, while total sales in the United States shrunk 16 percent between 1979 and 1980, the Japanese increased their sales by 6 percent during this period. The increase in market share by Japanese automakers came mostly at the expense of Chrysler and Ford. In addition, Volkswagen of America also surpassed American Motors in U.S. passenger car sales in 1979 after only a three-year production history in the United States. Finally, domestic sales of captive imports* increased from 1.8 percent to 2.5 percent in 1980. Most of these cars were manufactured

---

*Captive imports are cars such as the Buick Opel, Ford Fiesta, and Dodge Colt, produced outside the United States and Canada by subsidiaries of U.S. auto companies.

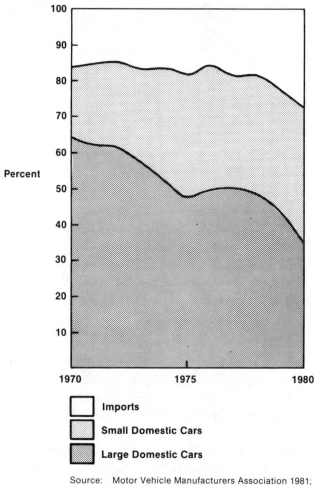

Source: Motor Vehicle Manufacturers Association 1981;
National Automobile Dealers Association 1981

Figure 1.2
Passenger Car Market Composition
(Percent of Retail Sales)

**Percent of
Domestic Market**

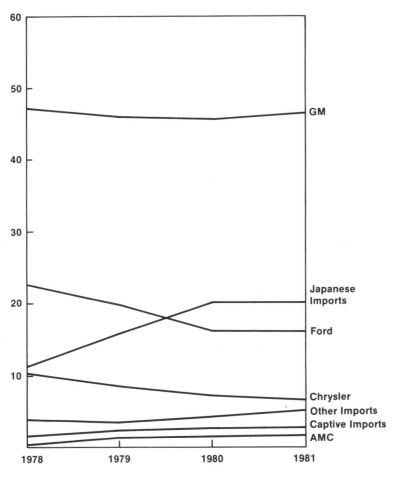

60			
50			GM
40			
30			
20			Japanese Imports
			Ford
10			Chrysler
			Other Imports
			Captive Imports
			AMC

1978   1979   1980   1981

Source: Motor Vehicle Manufacturers Association 1981, p. 12;
            National Automobile Dealers Association 1981, pp. 4-5;
            Automotive News, 1982

**Figure 1.3
Domestic Passenger Car Market Share**

11

in Japan. To make matters worse, the import share of the light truck market rose from 9 percent in 1978 to 22 percent in 1980. Sales of domestic makes plummeted from 3.3 million units in 1978 to 1.7 million units in 1980, a decline of 48 percent (Motor Vehicle Manufacturers Association 1981).*

By early 1980, Japanese imports became the prime target of the United Auto Workers, who with support from the Ford Motor Company, petitioned the federal government to restrict Japanese imports. Failing in their efforts to persuade a reluctant White House and Congress, they petitioned the International Trade Commission for relief from Japanese imports on the grounds that they were a major cause of serious injury to the U.S. motor vehicle industry.† In November 1980, after lengthy hearings, the Commission concluded that imports were not the principal cause of the industry's problems (U.S. International Trade Commission 1980). The Commission stated that although Japanese imports had aggravated the problem, the major cause was the sudden shift in consumer preference to small cars. The year 1980 thus ended with no help from the government.

Poor performance of the industry continued through 1981 and into 1982. Sales did not increase despite manufacturers' cash rebates, and by September 1981 interest rates had risen to 16 percent for new car financing, thwarting any possible recovery in sales. In contrast, the 1981 sales of imports increased slightly from previous years, and their share of the domestic market reached a new high of 30 percent in April. Nevertheless, U.S. firms managed to reduce their losses by rigorous cost cutting measures: layoffs, plant closings, wage and salary restraints, and negotiations with material suppliers.

In the spring of 1981 the Reagan administration reached an agreement with the Japanese government to restrict voluntarily their auto exports to the United States. The three-year agreement requires that in the first year, beginning in April of 1981, imports be limited to 1.68 million cars. (Japanese imports totaled 1.8 million units for 1980.) The limit was recently extended for the second year and is still left open for the third, and it will likely be tied to sales of

---

*In the rest of this book we limit our analysis to only passenger cars since most of our findings are equally valid for light and heavy trucks.

†The Trade Commission inquiry was instituted pursuant to Section 201(b) of the Trade Act of 1974 (19 U.S. Code 2251 b 1), which essentially allows domestic manufacturers to fight against dumping of products by foreign producers.

domestic cars. By the end of 1981 the new 1982 model domestic cars reached a record inventory supply of over 100 days. Three of the auto manufacturers reported losses for 1981: $1 billion for Ford, $470 million for Chrysler, and $137 million for American Motors. General Motors reported a profit of $333 million despite poor sales; this was due to the new tax law which allows corporations to trade unused tax credits. This law allowed cash-rich companies with larger tax liabilities to buy GM's assets and lease them back to the auto giant.

Poor performance and high unemployment in the industry led to a series of talks between the United Auto Workers and the U.S. auto firms. By the spring of 1982, the union had made wage and benefit concessions in return for job security and profit sharing. The agreement is expected to save Ford $1 billion over the next three years, and General Motors will be able to reduce their car prices by $300 per vehicle.

The dramatic and sustained drop in auto production in the United States has had serious consequences for the U.S. economy. The automobile industry consumes 21 percent of the nation's steel output, 60 percent of the synthetic rubber, 11 percent of the primary aluminum, 30 percent of the ferrous castings, 25 percent of the glass, and 20 percent of the machine tools (U.S. Department of Transportation 1981a). In addition, auto manufacturing contributes to employment, not only in the auto industry, but also in supplier and support industries. With the current unemployment rate of about 9 percent, we cannot afford a further drop in production at this time. It is clearly in the interests of the United States to support the auto industry until there is sufficient time for the economy to adjust to the structural changes brought about by the long-term decline in the manufacturing sector.

2

Past as a Prologue

The principal reason for the troubles faced by the domestic auto industry is its inability to change and adapt quickly to a shift in demand toward smaller cars. The industry, however, cannot be totally blamed for its inertia. After the Second World War growing affluence and cheap gasoline helped shape consumer preferences in the United States. The domestic auto industry capitalized on this preference by specializing in large cars. The difficulties in managing the current transition toward smaller cars is at the heart of the industry's financial problems. In this chapter we identify the major factors that have shaped the U.S. automobile industry.

The personal automobile is the second most expensive item in the household portfolio, next only to the home. It caused an unprecedented expansion in personal mobility and consequently influenced the patterns of living arrangements. It is an ultimate instrument for the enjoyment and expression of individual liberty, since control over when and how one gets from one place to another rests totally with the individual. The personal automobile has revolutionized lifestyles in the United States in less than three generations.

Ownership of passenger cars has doubled from 40 million units in 1950 to over 80 million by 1970. This growth is explained largely by the stable growth of the economy during the 1950s and 1960s and by the demographic changes brought about by the automobile itself. The spread of the personal automobile, economic growth, and demographic changes were mutually reinforcing factors.

In this chapter we shall examine how economic and demographic factors have influenced auto ownership over the last three decades. We shall also look at how these factors, as well as gasoline prices, consumer preferences, the emergence of automobile imports, and government regulations, have combined to produce our present situation.

THE POSTWAR ECONOMY

The postwar history of the U.S. economy can be conveniently divided into two periods: before and after 1970. The two decades between 1950 and 1970 were relatively tranquil in terms of inflation and unemployment rates. The U.S. economy grew between 1950 and 1970 at an average annual rate of 4 percent, twice the average rate for the 1970s. Not only were the average rates of economic performance better in the earlier decades, but also the fluctuations were less severe, particularly during the 1970s, which was one of the most affluent periods in U.S. history (Figure 2.1). The 1970s, on the other hand, were volatile, especially as sudden changes in the direction of the economy followed energy shortages.

Interest rate premiums demanded by lenders in the financial markets are one of the most striking differences between the 1950s and the 1970s. For instance, short-term interest rates were around 3 percent in the 1950s, 5 percent in the 1960s, and over 19 percent by mid-1981. Low interest rates of the first two decades after the war stimulated credit buying and significantly expanded the ownership of expensive durable goods, particularly automobiles. But economic growth and stability only partly explain the growth in automobile ownership. Demographic changes were equally important.

DEMOGRAPHIC FACTORS

As mentioned above, the high degree of mobility afforded by passenger cars profoundly influenced lifestyles in the United States. It accelerated suburbanization and made the automobile an indispensable item. The number of independent households rose from 43.5 million in 1950 to 63.5 million by 1970 — a rate faster than

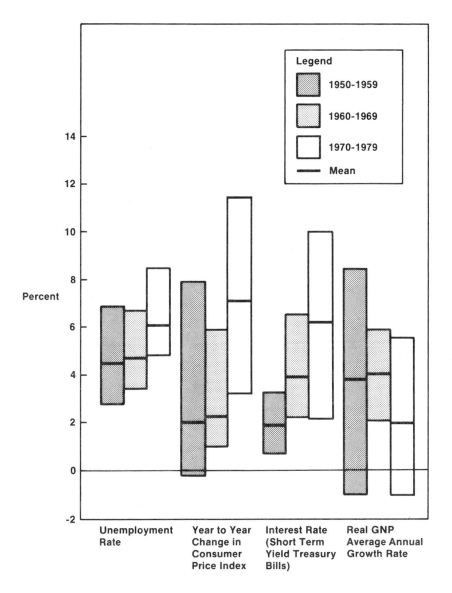

Source: U.S. Bureau of the Census 1980

Figure 2.1
The Mean and Range of Basic Economic Indicators

the rate of population growth. One of the obvious reasons for this phenomenon is that rising real income and low interest rates made it easier to fulfill what became known as "the American Dream": owning a home — which made the personal automobile an indispensable mode of transportation.

The growth in ownership of automobiles was accompanied by a growth in migration of population from rural to urban centers. The trend toward home ownership led to urban sprawl, suburban migration, and the need for multiple auto ownership. Such ownership increased the average number of cars per household from 0.8 in 1950 to 1.2 in 1970 (Figure 2.2). In 1960, 19 percent of all households owned two or more cars, while close to 25 percent did not own any car. By 1970, these values changed to 30 percent and 20 percent respectively. Half of all households now own two or more cars.

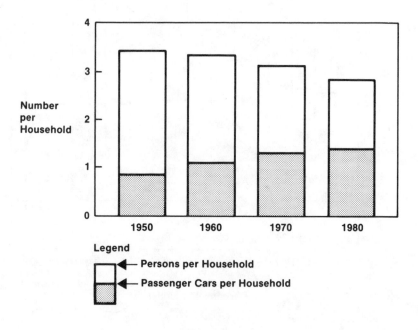

Source: U.S. Bureau of the Census 1980

Figure 2.2
Number of Cars per Household

Not only ownership but also the utilization of the automobile grew during this period (Figure 2.3). The number of licensed drivers grew at a faster rate than population. In 1950, only about 40 percent of the population were licensed drivers, but by 1970, this reached 50 percent. By 1970, 75 percent of all commuting trips to work were made by car. Over 67 percent of these were single passenger trips. Intercity travel, helped considerably by the interstate highway system, was almost totally dominated by the automobile. Of the one trillion intercity passenger miles travelled in 1970, 87 percent were made by car.

The Federal Aid Highway Act and the Highway Revenue Act of 1956 created the Highway Trust Fund. Revenues from excise taxes on automobile-related items were allocated to construction of the

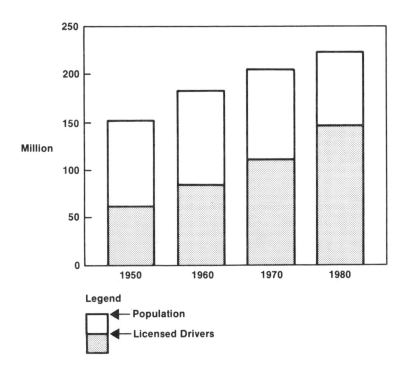

Source: U.S. Bureau of the Census 1980

Figure 2.3
Population and Licensed Drivers

40,000 mile Interstate Highway System. While the highway system helped intercity travel and freight movement, it was sold on the basis of satisfying the needs of national security by allowing rapid military mobilization. In addition to highways, the interconnecting network of secondary roadways helped link the rural areas to main highways. Only 59 percent of the 3.3 million miles of roads in 1950 were surfaced, but by 1970, close to 80 percent of the then 3.7 million miles were paved. These paved roadways helped the movement of agricultural products in rural areas.

The demand for surfaced roads increased and, in turn, stimulated use of the automobile and made the movement of population from inner cities to suburbs and from rural areas to metropolitan centers easier. In fact, improved roadways contributed to the general migration of population first from rural to urban and then from urban to suburban areas. In 1950, for instance, 64 percent of the population was located in urban areas. By 1970, it had increased to 74 percent. During the same period, suburban population increased from 20 to 27 percent of the total U.S. population. The outward movement of central city boundaries masks the level of postwar suburbanization suggesting that these figures may even be low.

GASOLINE PRICE

General economic conditions and demographic changes provide only part of the explanation for the increased ownership of automobiles. Another important factor was the price of gasoline. As shown in Figure 2.4, the number of vehicle miles traveled per licensed driver is responsive to gasoline price.* From 1950 to 1970 the price of gasoline actually declined in real terms, leading to a growth in vehicle use.

The price of gasoline has also been a major determinant of the type of car demanded by the public. In western Europe and Japan, high taxes have made the price of gasoline two to three times higher than in the United States. This, in addition to the geographic constraints in these countries, led to specialization in the design and

---

*Price elasticity estimates range around −0.3 (Greene 1981, p. 2-61). This means that a one percent decrease in gasoline price will result in a 0.3 percent increase in miles traveled.

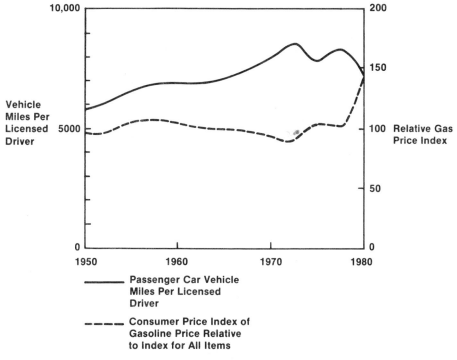

Source: Motor Vehicle Manufacturers Association, various issues;
Council of Economic Advisors 1981

Figure 2.4
Vehicle Miles Travelled and Gasoline Price

manufacture of small, fuel-efficient automobiles. In contrast, in the United States, low gasoline prices encouraged the demand for bigger automobiles with powerful engines. Thus, with the prospect of inexpensive gasoline, the average fuel efficiency of new cars declined throughout the 1960s from about 16 miles per gallon to 14 miles per gallon. Some of the large automobiles manufactured in the early 1970s had a fuel efficiency of as low as nine miles per gallon.

After 1973, however, the availability and the price of gasoline were subjected to severe jolts from the Organization of Petroleum Exporting Countries (OPEC) pricing policy and the responses of the U.S. government. This caused swings in consumer preferences through the 1970s (Figure 2.5). In 1971, President Nixon imposed economy-wide price controls which applied to gasoline and automobiles. In

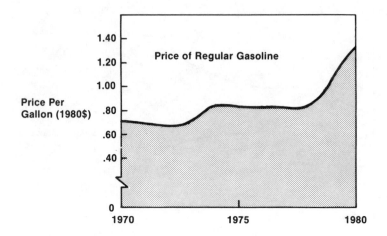

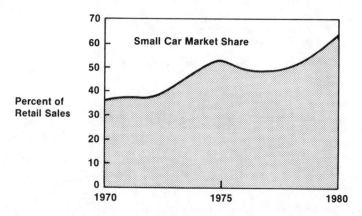

Source: Motor Vehicle Manufacturers Association, 1981;
          National Automobile Dealers Association 1981;
          Department of Energy 1981, p. 95

Figure 2.5
Gasoline Price and the Small Car Market

addition, his administration implemented monetary reform and allowed the U.S. dollar to float with respect to other currencies. The result was a negative balance in trade and a decline in the value of the dollar, which raised the price of imports. The market share of imported autos dropped for the first time in ten years. In 1973, the U.S. auto industry achieved the highest sales in its history. This came to an abrupt halt with the OPEC oil embargo in November 1973 following the Yom Kippur War between Israel and Egypt. OPEC successfully raised the price of imported oil from around $3 per barrel to $12 per barrel in a matter of months. As the price of gasoline climbed, so did the demand for small cars — from 43 percent of the market in 1973 to 53 percent in 1975. There is some evidence that the U.S. auto industry responded then with plans for an orderly conversion to smaller cars (Tucker 1980).

In December 1975 Congress passed the Energy Policy and Conservation Act and regulated the price of oil. For instance, this act called for a "roll back" of the price of domestic oil and limited the amount by which prices could increase in subsequent years. Based on the promise of continued inexpensive gasoline, the small car market share in 1976 declined for the first time in a decade. This trend continued until February 1979, when following the overthrow of the Shah, Iran shut down its oil production facilities. Worldwide gasoline supplies became short, pushing up the prices. The demand for small cars suddenly increased, and in 1980 small car sales accounted for over 60 percent of the market. The crisis of 1979 seems to have at last persuaded a skeptical public that future oil supplies from the Middle East are unreliable and higher gasoline prices are a fact.

THE INDUSTRY

In 1950, the U.S. auto industry produced 76 percent of all the passenger cars in the world, dominating the world market. Imports from England captured less than 10 percent of the U.S. market. Even in 1960, only 7.7 percent of the retail sales were made up of imports, mostly from Germany and England. However, imports from Germany were increasing and the Japanese were just beginning to market the Toyota line in the United States.

Despite a lack of competition from imports, the average real price of domestic automobiles has remained virtually constant, while the median family income of Americans has nearly doubled during the past three decades. For instance, it took 61 percent of the median family income in 1950 to purchase an average car. In 1970, it took only about 35 percent (Figure 2.6). Even during the 1970s, when real income was stagnant, the average retail price of a new car as a percent of median family income remained at 35 percent. This is attributed to the fact that the auto industry has been historically one of the most productive sectors of the U.S. economy.

Its success is mostly attributed to the economies of scale from mass production. The output per employee-hour, for instance, grew at an average annual rate of over 4.5 percent during the 1950s and the 1960s; whereas the average growth rate for all employed people in the private sector of the economy was only 3 percent per year (U.S. Department of Labor 1978). Even during the turbulent 1970s, auto industry productivity as measured by output per employee-hour grew at 2.3 percent per year compared to 1.4 percent for the whole private business sector of the economy. This enabled the auto industry to pay employees at well above the wage rates of workers in other manufacturing industries and to keep the prices of automobiles constant in real terms. It is estimated that by the end of

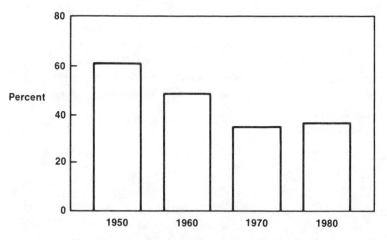

Source: U.S. Bureau of the Census 1980, p. 448; Motor Vehicle
Manufacturers Association 1981

Figure 2.6
Average New Car Price as a Percent of Median Family Income

1979, the average autoworker was paid 50 percent more per hour than the rest of the manufacturing workers (U.S. Department of Transportation 1981a).

Until the 1973 oil embargo, the general trend was toward performance, roominess, and luxury options in automobiles. The manufacturers made biennial introductions of new models, with minor technical or design modifications and major cosmetic changes. In the late 1950s, the huge tailfins of automobiles earned the contempt and ridicule of intellectuals who wrote about the affluent society and its problems. By 1972, the automobiles reached their peak in performance and weight, with an average new car fuel efficiency of around 12 miles per gallon. The demand for large cars allowed the domestic manufacturers to specialize in this segment of the market without competition from abroad. In the late 1960s, the most popular automobile was typically a sedan with a V-8 engine, two-barreled carburetor, air-conditioning, power steering, power brakes, and a radio. These options generally contributed to increased profits for both dealers and producers.

The profits and high wages enjoyed by the automobile industry were dependent upon a sustained demand for large U.S. cars. But as the 1970s proved, this trend did not continue as before; U.S. automakers were forced to compete with imports in the small car market.

Though imports have increasingly dominated the small car market, U.S. manufacturers have sold more small cars during the 1970s than foreign manufacturers in absolute terms (Figure 2.7). The poor performance by the industry during 1979 and 1980 was largely due to a drop in the demand for large cars, whereas the small car market continued its long-term growth pattern. This pattern began in the mid-1960s, long before the energy crisis. Detroit had experience with small cars as early as 1960, when the big three automakers introduced the Corvair (General Motors), the Falcon (Ford), and the Valiant (Chrysler) to compete with the highly successful Rambler, manufactured by American Motors. Ford introduced the Mustang in 1965, a small car which sold a record 470,000 units in its first year. In the 1970s, the industry, reacting to the increase in the small car market share, introduced the Vega and the Pinto. Unfortunately, both of these vehicles gained a reputation for being poorly engineered and assembled. When gasoline prices doubled in 1979, many consumers, looking for fuel economy and quality, turned to imports.

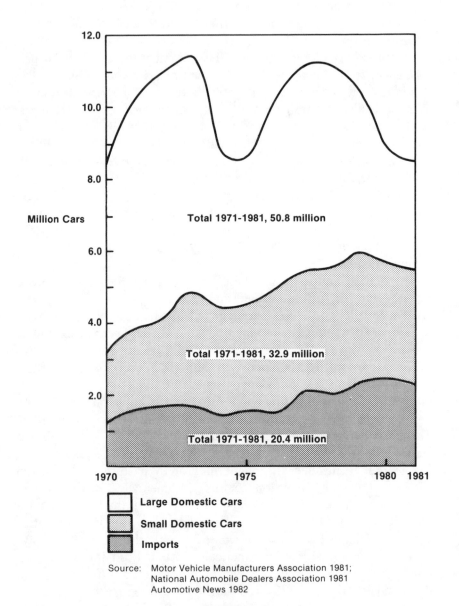

**Figure 2.7
U.S. Passenger Car Retail Sales**

Within the figure:

Million Cars

12.0

10.0

8.0

6.0

4.0

2.0

Total 1971-1981, 50.8 million

Total 1971-1981, 32.9 million

Total 1971-1981, 20.4 million

1970   1975   1980   1981

Large Domestic Cars

Small Domestic Cars

Imports

Source: Motor Vehicle Manufacturers Association 1981;
          National Automobile Dealers Association 1981
          Automotive News 1982

The principal emphasis of U.S. automakers has been on the large car market. In the past, the higher profit margins on large cars, made possible in part by limited competition from abroad, kept the domestic automakers from developing small cars for the future. But with current competition from Japanese importers, the U.S. automakers find themselves in a profit squeeze. It is estimated that the Japanese have a $1400 to $1500 per car landed cost advantage from lower wage-rates and higher productivity (Abernathy, Clark, and Kantrow 1981). Moreover, surveys show that consumers perceive Japanese automobiles to be of superior quality compared to domestic models (J. D. Power and Associates 1981).

REGULATIONS

During the 1970s, the auto industry came under increasingly costly and sometimes contradictory regulations relating to safety, auto emissions, and fuel economy (Lave 1981). When the safety of General Motor's Corvair was challenged by Ralph Nader, adverse publicity was triggered against many domestic makes. The consequent public pressures ushered in the era of safety regulations. The National Highway Traffic Safety Administration was created in 1966. This agency was charged with the responsibility of setting safety standards and with the power to require the recall of vehicles with safety defects. Later, after the energy crisis, this agency was also given the task of setting fuel-efficiency standards so that the trade-offs between safety and fuel efficiency would be considered in promulgating regulations.

In addition to safety, automobile emissions became an issue of serious concern during the mid-1960s. This concern was formalized with the Clean Air Act of 1970 and its subsequent amendments. As required by the Act, the U.S. Environmental Protection Agency established standards for emissions of carbon monoxide, hydrocarbons, and oxides of nitrogen.

These regulations, though controversial, have led to significant benefits. Partly as a result of safety regulations, the traffic fatality rates declined from five to three deaths per 10,000 motor vehicles between 1960 and 1980. Similarly, the number of cars with emission controls rose from 0 in 1960 to almost 99 percent of the 107 million cars on the road in 1980. On the cost side, estimates suggest that these regulations have added anywhere from $200 to $750 to the cost of a new car (Auto Hearings 1981). The costs may have been perceived as insignificant during affluent time, but at the present time they impose undue burdens on the industry.

SUMMARY

The post-World-War II evolution of the U.S. passenger car market suggests that cheap gasoline and the unprecedented affluence of the time favored the specialization of U.S. auto firms in large car production. This arrested the development of small cars which could now compete with the imports. The recurrent energy crises of the 1970s have permanently changed the structure of the U.S. automobile market in favor of small car producers. The U.S. auto industry currently faces a formidable challenge in this market from imports, particularly those that are made in Japan by well-managed firms employing low cost labor. In the following chapter we shall look at some of the global economic and demographic factors which are likely to determine the fate of the U.S. auto industry.

PART II

THE LONG-TERM
DECLINE

3

Labor Costs and
the Long-Term Decline

There is a widespread belief that the best way to preserve U.S. auto-related jobs is through lower wages. One of the most vocal critics of high wages is Roger B. Smith, Chairman of General Motors. He warns that,

> . . . if the labor costs should rise at a 10 percent average rate between now and 1985, they would approach $30 per hour. And if the Japanese also experience a 10 percent growth rate by 1985, their advantage would grow to nearly $12 per hour (over the current $8 advantage). . . . We cannot compete against any manufacturer who enjoys that kind of advantage over us. It is as simple as that. We are talking about saving jobs — American jobs. We're talking about this nation's principal industry . . . (General Motors 1981b).

Although Mr. Smith's warning is more of an illustration of the power of exponential growth than a statement of the current problem, there seems to be some validity to the point. For instance, recent estimates of the cost advantage enjoyed by Japanese imports range from $1400 to $1500 over comparable U.S. built cars (Abernathy, Clark, and Kantrow 1981; U.S. Department of Transportation 1981a). Although it is difficult to make strict wage comparisons, between 30 and 40 percent of this advantage appear to be due to lower wages and benefits of Japanese autoworkers; the rest is attributed to management performance. In recognition of this fact, the United Auto Workers have renegotiated their old contracts with Ford and General Motors and have conceded wage and benefit increases in return for profit sharing and job security.

In this chapter we posit that despite these wage concessions the long-term decline of automobile production in the United States is inevitable. The reason is that even with what amounts to an unprecedented concession of $2 to $3 per hour, U.S. autoworkers earn 25 percent more than Japanese and 80 percent more than Korean workers. The wage gap is simply too large to be closed by minor concessions. We have concluded that, in the face of international competition, there are three basic choices available to the U.S. government:

1. Continue to do nothing and simply preside over the decline of the U.S. auto industry and possibly face labor unrest from the persistent depression in auto-related industries.

2. Adopt a policy of economic isolationism by imposing local-content requirements and other trade barriers in an interdependent world and face loss of jobs in our growing export sectors from retaliation of our trading partners.

3. Negotiate an orderly transition toward a service sector economy through the development of human resources by implementing well-funded job training and worker relocation programs to help currently displaced labor.

We believe that the first option is unacceptable as it calls for the abandoning of legitimate duties of government in a civilized society. The second option will simply be counterproductive. The third option is the most prudent course for the U.S. government to follow during the next decade.

REASONS FOR THE DECLINE

The reason for these perhaps limited number of choices is that four important global economic and demographic factors, which are outside the control of the U.S. government, are likely to determine the future of industrial jobs in this country. First, U.S. automobile firms are either already multinational corporations or emerging in that direction rapidly. They do not need to locate their plants in this country, particularly now that they are competing intensely in the small-car market with producers from all over the world. Second, U.S. manufacturing labor has lost its advantage as being the most productive labor force in the world with the recent emergence of sophisticated and cheap labor of the developing nations.

Third, in stark contrast to the haphazard evolution of U.S. government policies toward industrial development, most foreign governments have systematically implemented incentives to attract multinational corporations. This is true particularly in the automobile industry because of its large economic multiplier effects. Fourth, there are very few new markets to absorb any increased world production of automobiles. As a consequence, the affluent, open market of the United States is likely to be a prime target for most exporting nations. We shall consider each of these four factors in detail.

Multinationals — The Active Agents of Change

The U.S. automobile industry consists of a group of emerging multinational corporations whose interests are not necessarily consistent with the interests of either the United States or its industrial labor force. These firms can move their production facilities outside of the United States to minimize their costs. Thus, they are active agents in the export of U.S. auto jobs. Historically, the U.S. labor force was insulated from competition from foreign labor by a lack of institutions which could easily move jobs across national boundaries. The multinationals aptly fill this role. For example, Ford Motor Company, which is truly a multinational, is the largest producer of automobiles outside of its home country: 50 percent of Ford cars and trucks were manufactured outside the United States in 1980 (Ford 1981a). Ford's operations outside the United States have accounted for an increasing share of its total revenues and earnings (Table 3.1). Ford manufactures cars in Germany, Great Britain, Spain, Canada, Brazil, Argentina, Australia, Mexico, South Africa, and other countries. Ford owns a 25 percent interest in Toyo Kogyo of Japan. Toyo Kogyo, incidentally, produces the Mazda line of automobiles and ranks as the fourth largest among U.S. importers.

TABLE 3.1
Ford Motor Company International Operations

Year	Dollar Sales Outside the United States as a Percent of Total Company Sales	After-Tax Return on Sales	
		United States	Outside United States
		(Percent)	
1980	50	*	2.5
1979	44	*	7.2
1978	35	2.9	5.3
1977	34	3.8	5.6
1976	37	2.4	5.4
1975	40	0.7	2.5
1974	35	1.1	2.3
1973	31	3.7	4.9
1972	31	4.5	4.2
1971	30	4.9	2.1

*Losses

Source: Ford Motor Company 1981b, p. 3.

General Motors, although not as successful as Ford in its international operations, produces over 1.5 million vehicles overseas each year – or one out of every five GM cars. GM plans to invest $8 billion, 18 percent of its total planned investments, outside of North America between 1980 and 1984 (General Motors 1981a). Currently, GM wholly or partly owns companies in 30 countries around the world which manufacture auto parts or assemble motor vehicles; it owns a 34 percent interest in Isuzu of Japan. Recently GM also announced the possibility of a joint venture with Toyota Motor Company of Japan.

Chrysler and American Motors have similar links overseas, though to a lesser degree than either Ford or GM. In 1980, for instance, Chrysler was the fifth largest importer of automobiles in the United States. Its imports are manufactured by its sister firm, the Mitsubishi Motor Corporation of Japan; Chrysler owns a 15 percent share of Mitsubishi. In 1980 the French government assumed virtual control of American Motors through its automotive arm, Renault, which owns 46 percent share of AMC.

Moreover, changes in the worldwide demand for automobiles has reinforced the growth of multinationals. What once was a segmented market, with U.S. consumers demanding large cars and the rest of the world demanding smaller cars, has become a homogeneous market with worldwide demand for virtually identical cars. The principal reason for this is the narrowing differences in gasoline prices paid by consumers. As a consequence, auto firms face stiff competition that drives them to seek centralization of operations and low cost labor and materials of developing countries. This intensifies the growth of multinationals.

The prime responsibility of the auto firms is to their stockholders. If it is more profitable to manufacture and assemble automobiles in Japan or Korea and sell them in the United States, that is what they can (and should) be expected to do. There is no compelling reason for the auto firms to continue operating within the United States rather than in Asia or South America. In this regard, the general sentiments of industry management are clearly reflected in the comments made by the Chairman of American Motors, Gerald Meyers:

> Economic goods will be built where the best labor quality situation occurs and if trade is free, and we believe in free trade, then it's very likely whatever has to be produced will be produced in the place where it can be the most competitive. This is not meant as a threat to the UAW or anybody else; it's a natural selection process. You just aren't going to be building something here at $20 an hour when it can be built at $12 an hour someplace else. (*Automotive News* November 9, 1981, p. E-12)

This is true not only for the auto industry but also for steel, glass, electronics, rubber, plastics, and other basic industries. The only exception here may be some of the defense-related industries which are required to operate within the United States for national security reasons.

Low Cost Foreign Labor

Historically the U.S. auto industry has enjoyed a near monopoly in world markets. For example, in 1950, 76 percent of the 10.6 million vehicles produced in the world were manufactured in the United States. In 1980 the United States produced about the same number of motor vehicles as in 1950, but its share of world production dropped to 21 percent (Motor Vehicle Manufacturers Association 1981, p. 7). During this same period, Europe increased its production by a factor of seven led by West Germany, France, Italy, Sweden, and the United Kingdom. Even more spectacular has been the growth in production in Asia (mostly in Japan) from 32,000 units in 1950 to over 11 million units in 1980.

These trends may have less to do with the loss of U.S. industrial leadership than with the growth of cheap technical manpower, particularly in Japan. In 1980 Japan surpassed the United States as the leading producer of automobiles. As shown in Figure 3.1 Japan and Spain, both with low labor costs, were the only auto manufacturing countries to increase production between 1978 and 1980. In addition, over half of the auto production of these two countries is exported while their imports are negligible.

Recently, many of the developing nations such as Malaysia, South Korea, Taiwan, Philippines, Singapore, India, Brazil, Mexico, Argentina, Chile, Venezuela, Greece, and Mainland China have all seen a growing population of technically sophisticated manpower available at as low as 10 percent of the hourly cost of U.S. autoworkers (Figure 3.2). Autoworkers in Brazil and South Korea earning less than 25 percent of the wages of U.S. workers pose a far more serious threat in the long term to U.S. labor than autoworkers in Japan earning less than 50 percent. Even though the quality of workmanship in these countries is currently not high, it is worth noting that it took less than a decade for Japan to rise from a poor to a very high quality of workmanship. Thus, any long-term solution to the unemployment problem in the U.S. auto industry through wage concessions will require up to a 400 percent reduction in domestic hourly wages.

Although the United Auto Workers are willing to negotiate to some extent, it is unlikely they will make such drastic concessions. The union will find it far more expedient to persuade the government to impose trade restrictions. For intance, before a congressional hearing in the fall of 1980 Douglas Fraser, President of the UAW, suggested: "A local content requirement is the best long term solution to the current problems plaguing the U.S. auto industry." (U.S. Congress, House. Committee on Ways and Means 1980, p. 37).

In addition to the fact that industrial labor is currently cheaper in the developing nations than in the United States it is likely to remain cheaper for a long time. This is due to both the growing

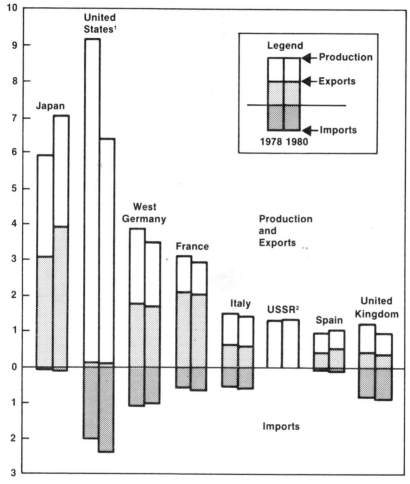

¹Does not include trade with Canada
²Import and export data not available

Source: Motor Vehicles Manufacturers Association 1980, 1981

**Figure 3.1
Exports and Imports for Top Eight Auto Manufacturing Countries
for 1978 and 1980**

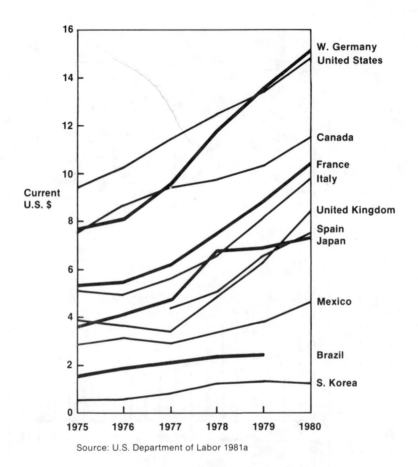

Source: U.S. Department of Labor 1981a

Figure 3.2
Estimated Hourly Compensation of Auto Workers
in Selected Countries 1975-1980

populations and the occupational transition from agricultural to manufacturing industries in these countries. During the last three decades, the fraction of the labor force employed in the industrial sector in most developed countries has either stabilized or declined while the same fraction has increased in the developing countries (Figure 3.3).

In contrast, the United States is undergoing a different type of occupational transition; namely, from industrial to service-oriented

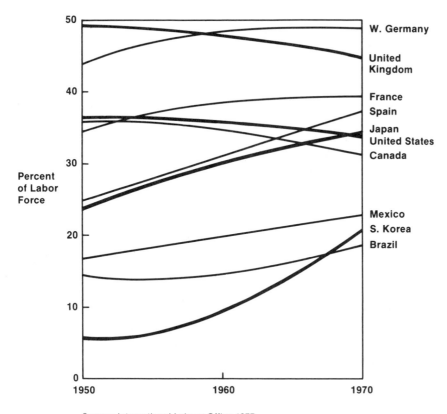

Source: International Labour Office 1977

Figure 3.3
Industrial Labor Force as a Percent of Total Labor Force
of Selected Countries

occupations (Ginzberg and Vojta 1981). The proportion of labor force employed in agriculture, mining, construction, and manufacturing dropped from 44 percent in 1950 to 29 percent in 1980. Furthermore, recent projections suggest that the U.S. labor force is not likely to grow during the coming decade at the same rate as in the 1960s and 1970s because the " . . . working-age population will be expanding much more slowly than during the 1970's (partly from) a protracted decline in birth-rates during the 1960's and the early 1970's." (Flaim and Fullerton 1978). Thus, the occupational transition away from manufacturing and mining jobs toward the service sectors combined with a slower growth of the labor force is likely to bid up the price of manufacturing and mining labor in the long term. This should only accelerate the trend in the relative decline of the manufacturing sector in the U.S. economy. For instance, the current slump in the auto industry is likely to make service sector and defense-related jobs relatively more attractive to domestic labor and thus create a long-term decline in the supply of skilled labor in automobile and other related industries.

Ideally, in a free labor market, cheap labor from the less developed countries will move into the lucrative U.S. market to bid the wages down. However, because of nationalist sentiments and tough immigration laws, the economic forces are not allowed to counter the existing disequilibrium in the international labor markets. In comparison to labor, capital and technology are relatively easy to move across national boundaries, especially for multinational corporations. Since we do not have a monolithic international union of industrial laborers, the multinationals can exploit the profit potential from wage differentials between various countries. Furthermore, because of high unemployment rates in developing nations, labor places very few demands on management. Often the very survival of individuals depends on jobs provided by the multinationals.

Industrial Policies of Other Nations

One of the important conclusions to emerge from a recent study by the Office of Technology Assessment (1981), a research arm of the U.S. Congress, is that the United States is perhaps the only developed nation in the world without any consistent national policy on commerce, industry, and technology. The current policy is a hodgepodge of lingering decisions of past administrations to impose politically popular tariffs and quotas. Briefly during the Carter Administration there were efforts to institute what was called a "reindustrialization" policy. It was simply a call for subsidies and special laws to help the failing industries in the Midwest. The Reagan Administration, in contrast, hopes to accomplish the revitalization of our industries through tax cuts and deregulation. Very little has been done, however, to investigate whether the steel, automobile, and electronics industries are strategically important for the United States or whether our nation should accept the growing economic dependence with other countries and the export of industrial jobs as inevitable trends.

Most nations pursue a deliberate policy of attracting industries to provide jobs. The developing nations in particular have elaborate incentives for attracting U.S. industries. The auto industry is one of the most coveted by these nations because of its material and labor intensive nature and the beneficial economic multiplier effects. For instance, in the United States one out of every six jobs is related to the automobile even though only one out of every one hundred jobs involves auto assembly. Also, since the auto industry demands large quantities of materials such as steel, glass, plastics, electronics, and rubber, it becomes economical to build large scale raw material plants. Thus, a poor nation with a growing supply of skilled labor such as Brazil can hope to develop its vast natural resources by creating a ready market for them in the auto industry.

Another important fact is that developing nations do not impose as many environmental and safety regulations which are perceived as stifling by auto firms. As the U.S. government pursued a policy of creating a safer, cleaner, and generally risk-free environment in the United States, it made it less and less profitable to conduct business here. This is particularly so in manufacturing and mining which generally entail greater risks than services.

Even relatively affluent nations which produce most of the automobiles in the world have adopted measures to protect their industries (Table 3.2). The Japanese automakers face stiffer barriers in Europe in comparison to the generous one year limit of 1.68 million units per year in the United States. In turn, Japan limits imports by indirect means such as very high dealer margins (often over 25 percent), Ministry of Transport requirements of hardware modifications, and a 5 percent higher commodity tax for larger cars (Comptroller General 1979, p. 38-56). For instance, a Ford Escort which in 1980 retailed for $7200 in the United States sold for about $11,400 in Japan. Moreover, bureaucratic delays in customs often add very heavy inventory cost penalties (*Far Eastern Economic Review* 1981, p. 54).

Developing nations protect their fledgling auto industries through high tariffs and local content requirements. With improved labor quality these requirements will become less and less binding on

TABLE 3.2

Automobile Trade Barriers of Major Auto Producing Nations in 1980

	Tariff	Local Content	Entry Restriction	Value Added Tax	Non-Tariff Barriers
United States	3%	None	Japanese limited to 1.68 million units	None	Strict safety emissions and fuel economy standards.
Japan	None	None	None	None	Strict emission standards. Difficult compliance procedures. Complex distribution systems. 5% higher commodity tax on large cars. Higher dealer margins on luxury (U.S.) cars.
W. Germany	10.9%	None	None	13%	Safety and emission standards. Tax based on horsepower.
France	10.9%	None	Japanese limited to 3% of market	33.3%	None
United Kingdom	10.9%	None	Japanese limited to about 10% of market	15%	None
Italy	10.9%	None	Japanese limited to 2200 cars	18-35%	Strict enforcement of "vehicle construction standards."
Brazil	Prohibited	Individually Determined	Determined by exports	11-44%	None
Mexico	35-100%	70%	Import license required	10%	None
Argentina	85%	75-96%	Import license required	16%	Miscellaneous charges.
Korea	150%	60-95%	Import license may be required	13%	Excise tax on gas of 180%.

Source: U.S. Department of Transportation 1981a, p. 52.

economic grounds since cheap labor would make it profitable to produce and assemble automobile components in these countries.

Sluggish Worldwide Demand for Cars

Foreign competition would not be a serious problem for U.S. labor if the worldwide demand for automobiles were to grow and absorb any increased output. The price of oil is likely to remain high, however, and dampen the demand for cars in most developing nations which depend on imported oil.

Moreover, Japanese motor vehicle production has been growing at an annual rate of 10 percent over the past five years. To sustain such a growth they must capture increasing shares of international markets, because their own domestic market is already saturated. The easiest and most lucrative target for them is the United States. Gasoline is still cheaper in the United States than in most other countries, and people are almost totally dependent on the automobile.

What is true of Japan today will most likely be true of the developing countries that lack large domestic markets for automobiles. Therefore, without growth in worldwide demand for automobiles, there is likely to be a rough one-to-one correspondence between jobs gained by foreign auto workers and jobs lost by the expensive U.S., German, and other Western European autoworkers.

In sum, these four global economic and demographic factors suggest that preserving U.S. auto jobs through wage restraints can at best be a short-term solution. In the following chapter we analyze this further, using a computer simulation model of the auto industry. We show the impact of minor versus major cuts in wage rates of U.S. autoworkers. It is unlikely, however, that major wage concessions will be made, and it can be reasonably assumed that the United Auto Workers will push for local-content requirements in the future. Douglas Fraser, President of the UAW, has specifically suggested a local-content requirement of 75 percent. This would require that at least 75 percent of the value of all automobiles manufactured in the United States come from domestic operations. This is an appealing policy as it promises to keep automobile-related jobs within the United States by forcing foreign manufacturers to move their plants to the United States. This policy also receives much support from supplier industries such as automobile parts, steel, rubber, plastics, aluminum, and electronics. In what follows we shall demonstrate the infeasibility of this policy and argue in favor of negotiating the current transition through a well-planned human capital development program.

THE INFEASIBILITY OF TRADE RESTRICTIONS

Is a local-content law likely to preserve U.S. auto jobs? The answer depends on how our trading partners respond. In this regard it is useful to review some facts on U.S. trade with other nations.

During the last three decades U.S. trade (imports and exports) with other nations has increased by a factor of 20 (Table 3.3). As a percent of our Gross National Product, U.S. exports have more than doubled from almost 4 percent in 1950 to over 8 percent in 1980.

Furthermore, U.S. trade is not restricted to developed nations alone. The trend of the 1970s suggests that the percent of U.S. trade with industrialized nations has gradually declined, while exports to nonindustrialized, even non-OPEC nations, have grown (Figure 3.4). The United States has increased trade of both agricultural and high technology items such as computers, machinery, and other consumer goods.

In turn, U.S. imports, dominated by oil from OPEC countries, have kept pace with the exports. The net result is that the U.S. economy is no longer as insulated from the world economy as it was even a decade ago. Interdependency among nations has grown

TABLE 3.3
U.S. Exports and Imports
(Million Dollars)

	Exports/GNP (Percent)	Exports	Imports	Net Balance
1950	3.6	10,203	9,081	1,122
1960	3.9	19,650	14,758	4,892
1970	4.3	42,469	39,866	2,603
1980	8.4	220,941e	249,185e	−28,244

e = estimates

Source: Council of Economic Advisors 1981.

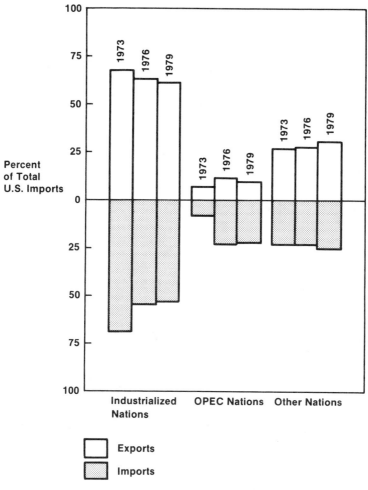

Percent
of Total
U.S. Imports

Industrialized Nations   OPEC Nations   Other Nations

☐ Exports

▨ Imports

Source: U.S. Bureau of the Census 1981

**Figure 3.4
U.S. Trade**

much during the post-World War II era, and the United States cannot afford to ignore the implications of its policies for the health of its exporting industries. Any protectionist measure implemented by the U.S. government is likely to provoke retaliation by other nations and may lead to unemployment in the export industries. Thus, we may be unable to protect our auto jobs without giving up jobs in other sectors such as agricultural machinery, computers, and, particularly, in the export of services. Therefore, it will be prudent in the long run to recognize the growing economic interdependency of nations and avoid short-sighted trade barriers.

Recognition of trade issues, though important for the long term, is hardly sufficient to help the unemployed autoworkers in the interim. There is an urgent need for a labor policy in this country which insulates individuals from the ravages of the market place — not simply a policy of subsidies and barriers to help preserve inefficient sectors — but one of retraining, rehabilitation, and job placement. West Germany has a similar policy to help the unemployed and those who seek change of careers where private firms are encouraged and subsidized to help train unemployed individuals.

HUMAN CAPITAL DEVELOPMENT

One of the relevant roles of government is to help develop "human capital" which consists of a healthy, motivated, and skilled labor force. Currently, tax credits, fast writeoffs, and an assorted set of subsidies are provided to stimulate investments in physical capital such as plant and equipment. But physical capital, without human capital to augment, will not be of much consequence. Human capital requires similar subsidies, particularly in the form of job training, and they can be justified on similar grounds as in the case of physical capital; namely, the benefits to society far outweigh the costs.

Human capital formation requires more than creating a physically and mentally healthy work force. It requires imparting of skills to understand and operate technologically complex and highly sophisticated capital goods. As the transition toward a service economy continues in the United States there will be an increasing need for highly trained professionals. This requires expensive institutions such as technical schools. Without a well planned and executed government policy, the coming decade may see much turmoil, especially among the domestic labor force in our basic industries.

One important policy is to help retrain unemployed autoworkers in high technology areas such as microcomputers, communications, and data processing. A second policy is to set up a comprehensive nationwide information system that matches available skills and jobs. In general, subsidies to firms which have training and information programs will help achieve human capital formation efficiently.

PART III
SHORT-TERM TRANSITION POLICIES

4

Influencing
Consumer Policies

In the last chapter we identified the global economic and demographic factors which are likely to lead to the long-term decline of the U.S. automobile industry. We argued that there is very little that the U.S. government could do to reinstate the industry to its former dominant role. This pessimistic outlook for the industry should not, however, deter from the fact that the currently displaced labor force needs government help in adjusting to the rapid changes in the industry's structure. In this and the following chapters we evaluate the relative merits of alternative short-term policies which are designed to help the auto industry cope with the current transition. By short term we mean the next three to five years during which the effects of various policies are likely to be fully manifest.

In this chapter we focus on the effects of four specific short-term policies that are frequently proposed. They are subsidies such as cash rebates or tax credits for the purchase of domestic cars, import quotas, wage concessions by workers passed on as price reductions to consumers (or alternatively rapid growth in productivity), and gasoline taxes. The first three of these are intended to help improve domestic new car sales and auto industry employment; the last policy is for stabilizing the demand for small cars by discouraging consumers from switching back to large cars as they did after the 1973 energy crisis. A common attribute of all four policies is that they are designed to influence consumer choices directly. Subsidies, wage cuts, and taxes, for instance, act through the price mechanism while import quotas simply restrict consumer options.

The primary concern in analyzing the relative merits of these policies is their impact on the stability of the short-term transition of the auto industry. Stability can be measured by the fluctuations of sales and employment over time. In this chapter we shall use the fluctuations in auto industry employment as the criterion variable for policy evaluation. In general, we do not favor policies which are likely to destabilize the industry further by causing unhealthy swings in sales and employment. For instance, if a certain policy boosts employment in one year followed by a severe depression the next year, we feel such a policy is not desirable.

METHODOLOGY

In order to test the sensitivity of new car sales and industry employment to changes in policies, future economic conditions, and other uncertain parameters, we developed a simulation model of the U.S. passenger car market called AUTO1. AUTO1 captures the basic elements of the supply-and-demand sectors of the automobile market. The model requires exogenous specifications of licensed drivers; gasoline prices; real per capita disposable income; capital, labor, and material costs of domestic auto firms; import car prices; new car fuel efficiencies; and the small car market share. It keeps track of the aggregate stocks of cars in use and the industry production capacity. AUTO1 explicitly models consumer choice between domestic and foreign new cars, new and used cars, and the investment decisions of the auto industry.

AUTO1 is not designed to forecast precise values of new car sales or employment, but used as a tool to study the fluctuations over time of domestic auto sales and employment in response to alternate assumptions. For instance, in Figure 4.1 the year-to-year fluctuations in auto industry employment are shown. These projections were made using the AUTO1 model by assuming three different growth rates in per capita real income, which is one of the most important variables influencing new car sales in the model (Table 4.1).* The base case represents, in our judgment, the likely evolution

---

*For interested readers a detailed presentation of the structure and assumptions of the AUTO1 model is provided in the appendix to this volume.

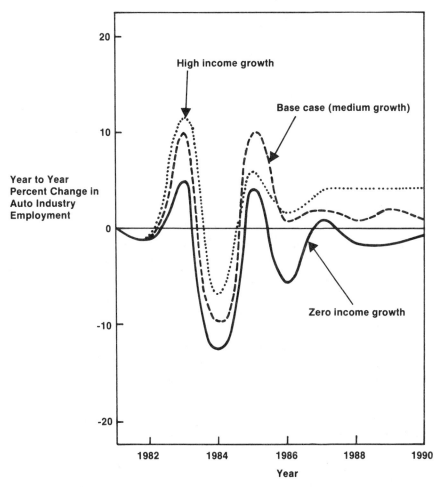

Source: AUTO1 Model Projections

Figure 4.1
The Effect of Different Income Assumptions
on Auto Industry Employment

TABLE 4.1
Assumptions on Real Disposable Income
(Percent Annual Growth Rate)

Year	Zero Growth	Base Case	High Growth
1960-70	–	3.1	–
1970-80	–	2.2	–
1980-82	0	0	0
1982-90	0	2.0	3.1

Source: Council of Economic Advisors 1981, p. 256; projections based on U.S. Department of Energy 1981, p. 103.

of the U.S. economy and the passenger car market during the rest of this decade. The high and low growth cases, respectively, represent optimistic and pessimistic income scenarios.

The projections shown in Figure 4.1 demonstrate the effect on auto employment of the current quota which limits Japanese imports to 1.68 million cars per year and is assumed to last for two years. These projections imply that as much as 10 percent of the auto manufacturing labor force in 1981, or about 45,000 workers, will regain their jobs due to the quota. When the quota is removed in 1983, however, these workers will again be laid off. This is clearly an undesirable behavior since the near-term transition is unstable. Thus, any new policy which either levels out these fluctuations or at least helps avoid future layoffs will be an improvement over the base case scenario represented in Figure 4.1. The base case thus offers a reference for comparing the relative effectiveness of alternative policies. A summary of results of the policy analysis using the AUTO1 model is presented in the following section.

SUMMARY OF FINDINGS

A continuation of direct consumer subsidies such as cash rebates (or tax credits) to promote sales and employment in the domestic auto industry is not a result of the AUTO1 model nor is such a continuation justified by historical experience. In fact, these subsidies may actually worsen the state of the auto industry by causing a boom-and-bust cycle in sales and employment. This effect can be particularly severe in a depressed economy as represented by our zero income growth assumption. Second, our analysis using the AUTO1 model suggests that import quotas can help only if they are set more tightly than now and extended for a longer period of time than the current two-year quota negotiated with the Japanese. Third, temporary wage concessions (such as the recently negotiated agreements by United Auto Workers and U.S. auto manufacturers), if passed on by the auto industry as savings to consumers, have virtually the identical effect as the temporary cash rebates. Drastic and permanent cuts in wages such as a 30 to 50 percent reduction from the current levels, however, will help increase sales and employment significantly. Fourth, a concerted effort by the U.S. auto industry to match the labor productivity of Japan can help domestic car sales, but, ironically, will not help labor as it will virtually freeze the employment at current depressed levels. Finally, a stiff 50 cent per gallon permanent tax on gasoline starting in 1983 causes a reduction of 1.2 million units in sales and costs close to 80,000 jobs. On the other hand, a 10 cent per gallon tax starting in 1983 is virtually harmless as a means of raising federal revenues, conserving on imported oil, and stabilizing the demand for small cars.

In the following sections we detail the analyses which led to the conclusions stated above. Whenever possible we like to use historical data to buttress our model results. However, with the exception of direct subsidies such as cash rebates there is very little historical information available on the response of U.S. auto sales and employment to various policies.

ANALYSIS OF HISTORICAL EXPERIENCE
WITH DIRECT SUBSIDIES

Direct subsidies influence consumer choices through the price mechanism. The subsidies can either be in the form of cash rebates and financing at lower than current rates or personal tax credits. In the former case, it is the stockholders who subsidize the consumers; whereas in the latter case it is the taxpayers who underwrite the subsidies. We address each of these separately.

Cash Rebates

Rebates are the most widely used form of subsidies. They act as temporary price reductions and are generally used to reduce inventories of new cars. Through most of 1981 and early 1982 rebates were used extensively by domestic automakers to spur sluggish sales of new cars. The rebate scheme rests on the general presumption that it will act as a pump-priming mechanism and unleash a "latent demand" for automobiles.

Rebates have been in use for a long time. Curiously enough, even though rebates entail administrative costs and are more complex than letting the retail car prices float with the dictates of supply and demand, the auto industry has always preferred rebates. Lawrence White explains that,

> The basic reason seems to be that the companies thereby gain flexibility and escape notoriety. The rebate programs can be granted and withdrawn quickly and quietly as the state of the market changes, without having to attract the attention of the press and of Washington by changes in list prices; price cuts can be achieved on particular models with no explanations to reporters about those models that have been selling poorly, thereby avoiding the impression that there is something wrong with those models and deterring other customers. Also, at the transition from one model year to the next, the increase in list prices, if any, will be less under the current system than if list prices floated at the end of the model year along with actual prices. (White 1971, pp. 119-120)

Have cash rebates helped the auto industry? Under normal economic conditions it is possible to justify cash rebates for clearing inventories of old models in dealer showrooms to make room for the newer models. History, however, does not lend support to the scheme of cash rebates to boost new car sales in a depressed economy. In general, rebates seem to create temporary booms in sales only to be followed by a bust.

In Figure 4.2, the monthly new car sales are shown for two of the worst periods for our economy (1974-75 and 1980-81) since World War II. Cash rebates were offered intermittently during these two periods by all four domestic auto firms. In order to adjust for seasonal variations, new car sales are shown as a percent of sales for the same month in the previous years and also as a percent of

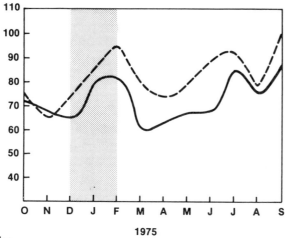

**Monthly Sales
(Percent)**

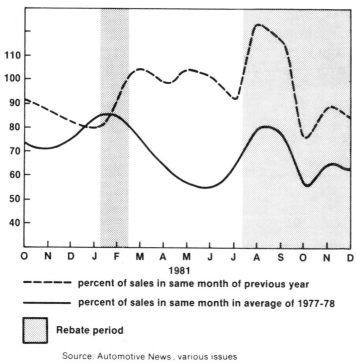

- - - - - percent of sales in same month of previous year

——— percent of sales in same month in average of 1977-78

Rebate period

Source: Automotive News, various issues

**Figure 4.2
Experience with Cash Rebates by the Auto Industry**

average sales in the same month during two of the best years in recent history (1977 and 1978). The magnitude of the rebates varied between 5 and 10 percent of the retail prices. The shaded region in Figure 4.1 indicates the approximate duration of the rebates. The typical sales behavior displayed in this figure is a rapid rise in sales in response to rebates followed by a slump.

During the summer of 1974, following the OPEC oil embargo, economic conditions began to deteriorate. The usual October (new model) sales peak failed to occur. By January 1975, when the economy was in the grip of the worst postwar recession, automobile inventories reached a high level of 90 days of supply compared to a normal level of 60 days. The industry responded with cash rebates in January 1975 that lasted until the end of February. The daily selling rate of new domestic cars rose to 22,321 from the January level of 17,796 but slumped again in March to 20,130 units (Wards 1976, p. 119).

The experience during 1981 was quite similar. Despite intense rebate campaigns throughout 1981, new car inventories reached a peak of 100 days of supply by the end of October and have remained at this record level through the spring of 1982. The new 1982 models did very little to boost consumer demand. The lesson to be learned is that during periods of high unemployment and a stagnant economy, rebates offer little help to the auto industry except to hold down inventories of new cars which the auto industry could have avoided producing in the first place.

The reason for the ineffectiveness of rebates is that during depressed times the poor prospects of future income depresses consumer expenditures for durable goods such as automobiles. Therefore, cash rebates must be substantial and offered for prolonged periods of time to offset the negative effects of the poor economy on consumer confidence. Even then it might not help new car sales as is eminently proven by the 1981-82 rebates. At best, rebates boost sales temporarily only to be followed by a slump. Thus, auto firms, in responding to pressures to hold down inventory costs, may be unwittingly cannibalizing their own market. Rebates poorly serve the stockholders in auto firms since it merely transfers their wealth to consumers.

Tax Credits

Rebates provided by the government take the form of tax credits. In this case the auto buyers gain at the expense of taxpayers rather than the stockholders as in the case of rebates. Perhaps for this reason, Chrysler Corporation proposed the National Automotive Recovery Act in 1981, the centerpiece of which is a personal tax credit for the purchase of U.S. built cars (Chrysler 1981, p. 4). Even more specific was Senator Dan Quayle of Indiana, who in order to help the auto supplier industry in his state, proposed a $750 personal tax credit for buying U.S. built cars (Auto Hearings 1981, p. 75).

He justified this proposal by suggesting that the U.S. Treasury can actually make a profit from increased tax revenues and foregone unemployment compensation offsetting the revenue loss from tax credits. He assumed the short-term price elasticity* of demand for automobiles to be −2.5, a very high value compared to some of the recent estimates which cluster around −0.6 (Table 4.2). If Senator Quayle's assumptions were correct there would be no need for tax credits since the auto companies could use cash rebates to their advantage by offering a 10 percent cash rebate and increasing their sales by 25 percent. This would improve plant utilization, help reduce unit costs, and boost profits. As recent history has shown, however, rebates have not led to miracles, which only suggests that price elasticity of demand is much lower than what Senator Quayle assumed.

TABLE 4.2
Short Run New Car Demand Elasticity Estimates

Study	*Year*	*Price Elasticity*	*Income Elasticity*
Chase Econometrics	1974	−0.88	n.a.
Transportation Systems Center	1974	−0.60	1.93
Energy and Environmental Analysis, Inc.	1975	−0.20	n.a.
Sweeney/Stanford	1979	−0.64	2.3

Source: Chase Econometrics 1974; Schuessler and Smith 1974; Energy and Environmental Analysis, Inc. 1975; Sweeney 1979.

---

*Price elasticity of demand denotes the percent change in quantity demanded for a 1 percent change in price.

Analysis of the tax-credit option using the AUTO1 model lends further support to our position that subsidies can actually destabilize the near-term transition by causing unhealthy swings in sales and employment.

POLICY TESTS WITH AUTO1 MODEL

10 Percent Tax Credit

We used the AUTO1 model first to determine the effects of a one year, 10 percent tax credit offered in 1982 to consumers for the purchase of domestic automobiles. In the model the tax subsidy helps improve sales by lowering the annualized cost of owning and operating new domestic cars. We use an estimated value of −1.99 as the elasticity of demand with respect to the annualized costs, which roughly translates to a price elasticity of demand of −1. The sudden boost in new car demand sets in motion a chain of events within the AUTO1 model which result in increased capacity utilization and lower inventories which result in lower unit costs. For instance, a 10 percent tax credit on an $8,500 automobile actually results in a $1,000 savings per car to the consumer, which increases new domestic car demand by 1.5 million units in 1982 over and above the base case sales of 8 million units. It should be remembered that the tax credit was superimposed on the import quota on Japanese cars already in force. The net result is that in 1982, 110,000 autoworkers will regain employment from a 10 percent tax credit.

But when the tax credit is removed in 1983, the model results suggest a precipitous decline in sales of about 1.4 million units leading to a layoff of 107,000 workers. Figure 2.3 illustrates this destabilizing effect of tax subsidies. The percent change in employment from the previous year swings from 20 percent in 1982 to −20 percent in 1983 due to the tax subsidy, which is much more severe compared to the plus or minus 10 percent under the base case. Thus, rather than improve on the base case behavior, the tax credit actually makes things worse for the autoworkers.

Since the tax credit was superimposed on top of the import quota, the effects on employment may be exaggerated. We also tested a case where tax credits become effective in April 1983, after the expiration of quota. The model results from this are also shown in Figure 4.3. As can be seen, the behavior of auto employment improves significantly over the base case. This suggests that timing may be an important variable in providing consumer subsidies.

In order to illustrate how tax subsidies can lead to even more severe instabilities in a low growth economy, we tested two one year, 10 percent tax-credit policies under the assumption of zero income growth. The results are plotted in Figure 4.4. In the first case, with the tax credit in 1982 coinciding with the import quota, the post-tax-credit period shows a much more severe drop in employment in 1983 than was illustrated in Figure 4.3. If the tax credit follows the removal of the import quota, it is effective in postponing the problem of layoffs and unemployment until 1985, but, unlike the base case with moderate income growth, does not remove the instability. This lends credence to our earlier statements about the ineffectiveness of direct subsidies in undoing the effects of a stagnant economy.

Import Quotas

In April 1981, the Reagan Administration successfully negotiated a "voluntary restraint" agreement with the Japanese auto exporters. The agreement is a de facto quota on Japanese made cars imported into the United States limiting them to 1.68 million units per year for two years, a reduction of 0.23 million units per year from the 1980 level. Has the quota helped? Would the auto industry have been better off without a quota? Or do we need more stringent limits on imports extended for a longer period of time? These are questions we address in this section. For lack of adequate empirical information, we used the AUTO1 model to study the impacts of alternative quotas.

As we mentioned earlier, the base case projections already incorporate a two year quota in which we limit the total of all imports to 2.2 million units. This 2.2 million limit assumes that during these two years 1.68 million units of Japanese cars and 0.52 million units of non-Japanese cars will be imported into the United States. In other words, we have assumed that imports from Europe will capture very little of the lost Japanese sales. We tested the following three cases using the AUTO1 model.

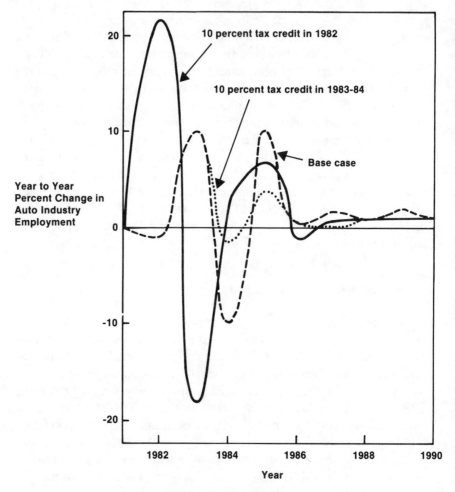

20 —

10 percent tax credit in 1982

10 percent tax credit in 1983-84

10 —

**Year to Year
Percent Change in
Auto Industry
Employment**

Base case

0 —

-10 —

-20 —

1982   1984   1986   1988   1990

Year

Source: AUTO1 Model Projections

**Figure 4.3
The Effect of a One Year Personal Tax Credit with
Moderate Income Growth on Auto Industry Employment**

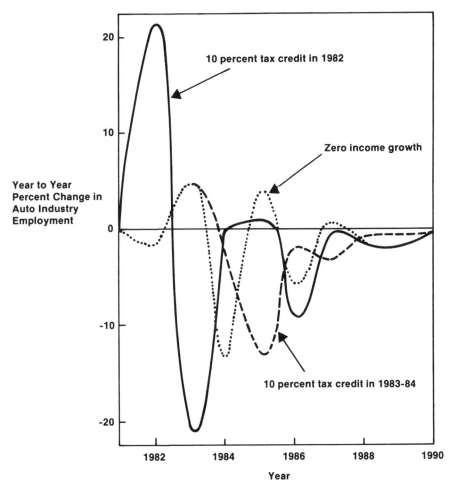

Year to Year Percent Change in Auto Industry Employment

10 percent tax credit in 1982

Zero income growth

10 percent tax credit in 1983-84

Year

Source: AUTO1 Model Projections

Figure 4.4
The Effect of a One Year Personal Tax Credit with
Zero Income Growth on Auto Industry Employment

1. No quota
2. 2 million unit per year quota on all imports from April 1981 to 1990.
3. 1 million unit per year quota on all imports from April 1981 to 1990.

The results in terms of the year-to-year percent change in employment are plotted in Figure 4.5 along with the results for the base case. First, it is clear that if the current quota were not in force, U.S. autoworkers would have suffered additional unemployment of 10 percent of the labor force (about 45,000 workers) in 1982. The temporary quota simply shifts this unemployment to 1984, when, as indicated by the base case, 10 percent of the autoworkers will be laid off. Only a sustained quota is able to solve this problem. As indicated in the figure, both the two million and the one million unit quota cases stabilize the transition by shifting the percent change curve completely above the zero level. This implies that these policies will lead to a sustained growth in U.S. auto employment. As we argued in the last chapter, however, sustained quotas are tantamount to a long-term, local-content regulation; and they may not be feasible politically.

Wage Concessions and Productivity Growth

In the spring of 1982, after weathering a severe depression in the previous quarter, the United Auto Workers renegotiated their old wage contracts with Ford and General Motors. In return for job security and profit sharing, the autoworkers gave up wage increases and certain fringe benefits, at least temporarily. This unprecedented agreement is expected to save over $2 billion for each of the two manufacturers.

We tested the effect of these concessions on the growth of auto industry employment, assuming that all savings will be passed on to consumers. Temporary concessions led to the same problems as temporary tax credits; they caused severe instability in auto employment in the near term. In fact our analysis suggests that even drastic long-term wage concessions do not help improve the near-term instability in employment represented by the base case (see Figure 4.1). Permanent wage cuts, however, do help improve the long-term growth in auto jobs.

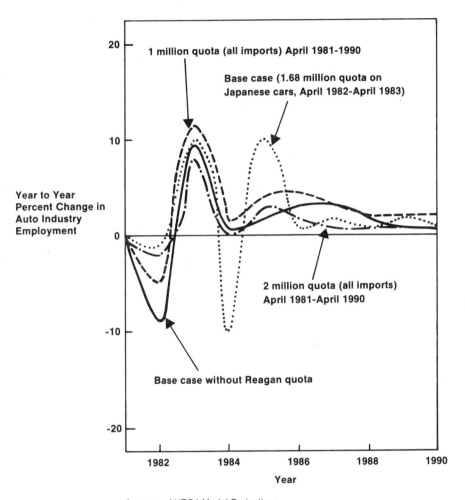

Source: AUTO1 Model Projections

**Figure 4.5
The Effect of Import Quotas on Auto Industry Employment**

65

We tested the effects of three different future wage paths shown on the top section of Table 4.3. In all these cases we assumed the wages to remain constant beyond 1985. Although our assumptions of future wage cuts may seem implausible and unfair, it is worthwhile comparing the autoworker's wages with those of other comparably skilled workers. For this purpose, the wages of the average U.S. manufacturing worker and the Japanese autoworker are shown in the lower half of Table 4.3. In 1980, the U.S. autoworkers earned 50 percent higher wages than the average U.S. manufacturing worker and over twice that of Japanese autoworkers. Assuming that all these wages continue to grow at about 1.8 percent per year, based on recent trends, the U.S. autoworker would still maintain the same relative advantage in 1985 as in 1980. Thus, even a 50 percent cut in wages between 1980 and 1985, as we assume in one of our cases, makes the U.S. autoworker just competitive with the Japanese autoworker.

The results from the AUTO1 model are shown in Table 4.4. When we hold productivity growth constant at an average rate of 1.54 percent per year, and vary the wage rates, we find that even a

TABLE 4.3
Comparison of Assumptions on Real Hourly Compensation
(1980$/hour)

	1980	1985
Wage Case 1:		
U.S. Autoworker		
Constant real wages	15.00	15.00
Wage Case 2:		
U.S. Autoworker		
30% decline between 1980 and 1985	15.00	10.50
Wage Case 3:		
U.S. Autoworker		
50% decline between 1980 and 1985	15.00	7.50
U.S. Manufacturing with a 1.8% annual real increase	10.00	10.93
Japanese Autoworker with a 1.8% annual real increase	7.00	7.65
U.S. Autoworker with a 1.8% annual real increase		
(base case)	15.00	16.40

Source: Estimated by Authors.

TABLE 4.4
The Effect of Wage Reductions and Productivity Growth on
Auto Industry Employment
        (Average Growth Rates in Percent Per Year)

Test Cases	Assumptions		Model Results
	Wage Growth	Productivity Growth	Auto Industry Employment Growth
1. Base Case			
1982-90	1.67	1.54	1.50
2. Wage Case 1			
1982-90	.00	1.54	2.40
3. Wage Case 2			
1982-85	−5.75	1.54	4.80
1985-90	.00	1.54	2.40
4. Wage Case 3			
1982-85	−13.90	1.54	5.00
1985-90	.00	1.54	2.50
5. Productivity Case			
1982-90	1.67	4.42	.00

Source: Assumptions were based on recent industry trends and the employment impacts were projected using the AUTO1 model.

5.75 percent annual reduction in real wages between 1982 and 1985 causes the employment to grow at 4.8 percent per year. This means 25,000 new jobs will be added each year due to a 30 percent decline in real wages by 1985. More than doubling the rate of reduction in real wages, as implied by the 13.9 percent per year decline case, does not seem to add appreciably to the growth in auto industry jobs, suggesting diminishing returns to wage cuts. An interesting point is that even a wage freeze imposed in 1982 for eight years would add over 5000 more autoworkers to the payroll each year than under the base case. Thus, there are definitely benefits to be reaped from lowering autoworkers' wages to the levels of workers in other manufacturing industries in the United States. Although this may not help improve the stability of the transition, it will at least help slow down the rate of decline of the auto industry employment.

We also tested a productivity case in which the wage rate is assumed to grow at 1.67 percent per year as in the base case. Furthermore, the average annual growth rate in output per laborhour grows at 4.42 percent per year between 1982 and 1990, which is at over three times the rate of the base case. This assumption implies that the number of laborhours required per car declines from 140 in 1980 to 90 in 1990, compared to our base case assumption of 120 hours by 1990 for the same level of sales. In comparison, the current Japanese productivity is estimated to be around 80 laborhours per car (Abernathy, Clark, and Kantrow 1981).

The AUTO1 model results, shown at the bottom of Table 4.4., indicate that an accelerated growth in productivity will freeze the number of jobs in the auto industry at current depressed levels. Productivity growth is the most likely future path of the auto industry. Even a wage freeze or drastic concessions may not make labor attractive enough to slow down the rate of substitution of capital for labor in the auto industry. In practical terms, this means that higher productivity will offset the need for additional labor. Further, robots and other automated equipment will replace labor in the auto production plants as U.S. automakers use the newest automated technology to compete internationally.

Gasoline Taxes

The reason why European and Japanese automakers make better small cars than U.S. automakers is that they have historically catered to consumers who have consistently preferred small cars because of the relatively high gasoline prices in Europe and Japan. In Table 4.5 the price of regular gasoline and taxes for the United States and five other countries are shown. In 1980, for example, tax rates in European countries and Japan were three to five times the tax rate in the United States. Thus, one way to ensure that consumers in the United States will consistently prefer small cars is to set a price floor, or alternatively, impose gasoline taxes. A stable market for small cars will help preserve the large investments made by the U.S. auto industry in small car production capacity. The recent decline in the world price of oil has rekindled fears among domestic auto firms that consumers may revert back to demanding large cars as they did after the oil crisis of 1974. In addition to stabilizing the small car market, gasoline taxes are frequently suggested as a way of raising federal revenues for the repair of our

TABLE 4.5
Price of Regular Gasoline in Selected Countries in March 1980

Country	*1980 Dollars per Gallon*	*Percent Tax*
United States	1.20	11.7
France	2.84	63.0
Italy	3.18	68.9
United Kingdom	2.44	44.4
Germany	2.31	55.0
Japan	3.14	40.0

Source: Motor Vehicle Manufacturers Association 1981, p. 32.

national highways. Furthermore, it will help conserve imported oil. Using the AUTO1 model we determined the impacts of two different levels of gasoline taxes; namely, a 10 cent per gallon and a 50 cent per gallon permanent tax starting in 1983.

The test results are shown in Table 4.6. Both the first year and the long-term response to the gasoline taxes are shown in terms of

TABLE 4.6
The Major Benefits and Costs from Gasoline Taxes

Test Cases	*Benefits*		*Costs*
	Gasoline Savings (Billion Gallons/Year)	*Government Revenues (Billions of 1980 Dollars/Year)*	*Jobs lost in Auto Industry (Persons/Year)*
1. 10 cent per Gallon Tax From 1983-90			
a. First Year Response	2.00	6.00	13,000
b. Permanent Response	1.50	5.00	7,000
2. 50 cent per Gallon Tax From 1983-90			
a. First Year Response	7.40	30.00	78,000
b. Permanent Response	5.50	23.00	25,000

Source: AUTO1 Model Projections.

three important variables: gasoline savings, federal revenues, and loss of jobs. A 10 cent per gallon tax is expected to lead to a loss of 13,000 jobs in the auto industry due to reduced car sales which were projected to decline in the first year by 220,000 units. The first year benefits of the 10 cent tax are savings of 2 billion gallons of gasoline (3 percent of our current use) and $6 billion in increased federal revenues. The short-term effects from a 50 cent per gallon tax are much more severe, leading to a loss of 78,000 jobs or close to 20 percent of the currently employed autoworkers.

The long-term annual rate of loss of jobs, though much lower than the first year effects, is still severe under the 50 cent per gallon case. On the benefit side, a 50 cent tax would displace the need for one large synthetic fuel (coal liquid) plant producing .5 million barrels per day of oil. Moreover, increased federal revenues will average about $23 billion per year, which can be put to good use in improving our national transportation systems.

On the issue of stability, the gasoline taxes do not have an appreciable impact on the year-to-year change in auto employment or sales in the next three to four years. Thus, on the basis of costs and benefits summarized in Table 4.6, the 10 cent per gallon tax may be tolerable while the 50 cent tax may place an excessive burden on the autoworkers. The optimal tax may lie somewhere between these extremes, and it is an area requiring careful study of the secondary and tertiary effects that are beyond the capability of the AUTO1 model.

5

Industry Subsidies: Are They Necessary?

One of the most appealing short-term government policies in support of the U.S. auto firms is to subsidize the financing of new automobile plants to produce small cars that can compete with Japanese imports. In this chapter, we evaluate the merits of such proposals and conclude that domestic auto firms do not need any government assistance since capital does not appear to be the constraining factor in the restoration of the industry (Abernathy, Clark, and Kantrow 1981; Harbour 1981). With the exception of Chrysler Corporation, U.S. auto firms have been able to raise the necessary capital even in bad years. Nevertheless, their ability to continue as before may be in jeopardy unless their recently introduced small models sell in large numbers. The industry will be hard pressed in justifying new capital plants without such sales increases.

The argument supporting government subsidies is generally based on the following line of reasoning: the industry is in bad shape and cannot raise investment funds in the capital markets, and unless they build new plants to produce cars that are competitive they will decline further. Government must help the industry out of this vicious cycle. Implicit in this argument is the following set of questionable assumptions:

1. Competitive new cars are currently not being built, because the U.S. auto firms lack domestic new plants and equipment. If the

auto industry had the capital to build these plants, they could become profitable.

2. The investment requirements are too large [a U.S. Department of Transportation (1981a, p. 64) estimate places it at $70 billion between 1979 and 1985] for auto firms to finance, especially when they are losing money.

3. The existing tax incentives are not sufficient to help the industry raise the necessary capital.

4. Subsidizing the depressed automobile firms is one of the better opportunities for allocating tax revenues to reduce unemployment among autoworkers.

We shall consider each of these and show that facts contradict the first two assumptions and lend only minimal support for the latter two.

NO NEED FOR NEW PLANTS

Between 1979 and 1982 the big three U.S. automakers introduced small, front-wheel drive automobiles: General Motors' X and J cars, Ford's Escort and Lynx, and Chrysler's K cars. These new models, which are designed to compete with the small Japanese imports, have not yet returned the industry to profitability. The market share lost to Japanese imports has not been recaptured. Domestic new car inventories reached a record level of 107 days of supply by January 1, 1982, (Table 5.1) which is almost twice the typical level of 60 days and 80 percent over the level a year ago. This occurred despite the fact that cash rebates as high as 10 percent were offered by U.S. automakers throughout most of 1981. When current levels are compared with inventory levels a year before the case appears even worse. On the basis of inventories the domestic large cars accounted for less than half of all the unsold cars, faring much better than the small cars.

This is partly due to the fact that the prevailing interest rates which have been between 15 and 20 percent and the current recession have depressed overall auto sales. It is also due to the high price of domestic small cars relative to the price of Japanese imports; estimates place the differences at $1400 to $1500 for comparable cars (Abernathy, Clark, and Kantrow 1981).

TABLE 5.1
Domestic New Car Inventories by Size Class

	Days Supply			Distribution (Percent)	
Size Class	Jan. 1, 1982	Jan. 1, 1981	Percent Increase	Jan. 1, 1982	Jan. 1, 1981
Subcompact	149	83	80	30	22
Compact	106	81	31	24	30
Intermediate	120	91	32	30	32
Standard	66	65	2	11	12
Luxury	81	44	94	5	4
All Cars	*107*	*80*	*34*	*100*	*100*

Source: Automotive News, January 19, 1981 and January 18, 1982.

Thus, lack of small car production capacity cannot be blamed for the poor showing of auto industry profits. Rather, it is the poor economy and the high price of domestic cars relative to imports which are the sources of the current problem.

INDUSTRY INVESTMENT REQUIREMENTS

The U.S. Department of Transportation (1981a) recently estimated that over $70 billion in 1980 dollars will be required for the U.S. auto industry to meet its production plans between 1979 and 1985. (Also see Shackson and Leach 1980.) The report states that $70 billion would be "the largest privately funded program in history, dwarfing the Alaskan pipeline and even the government's Apollo program." The estimate is based on the assumption that a 12 million unit capacity of front-wheel drive cars, trucks, and vans is needed by 1985. This is an unrealistic assumption since the current capacity of about 5 million front-wheel drive vehicles is being utilized at less than 60 percent.

There is currently little reason for rapid expansion in production capacity given the fact that the domestic automakers are not able to sell all of their front-wheel drive, four-cylinder cars today without resorting to cash rebates and heavy advertising. Projecting investment requirements based on a 12 million unit capacity can therefore be merely a tentative estimate. Even General Motors, which had planned to spend $35 billion between 1980 and 1985, is currently revising its spending downward. Thus, a more realistic estimate of capital requirement for the industry is $50 billion between 1979 and 1985, or about the same as the industry's investment between 1975 and 1980 (Table 5.2). Although $50 billion may still be larger than either the Apollo program or the Alaskan oil pipeline investments, it is well within the range of previous investments made by the auto industry. Even though 1980 was one of the worst years for the auto industry, $11.45 billion was spent on new auto plants and equipment. At this rate even a $70 billion investment by 1985 seems within the reach of the industry. Thus, the assumption that investment demands are too large for the auto industry is unrealistic on the grounds that the industry is unable to utilize fully its existing small car production capacity.

Furthermore, facts indicate that financing new investments may not be a serious problem. During the 1970s for instance, some of the largest investments have been financed by the auto industry during the worst years; in fact, investments appear to be inversely related to earnings (Figure 5.1). A quarter of all the capital investments

TABLE 5.2
Capital Expenditures of Major Auto Firms in the United States
(Billions of 1980 Dollars)

Year	GM	Ford	Chrysler	AMC	Total	Percentage of Decade
1971	3.4	2.1	0.5	0.1	6.1	8
1972	3.7	2.3	0.6	0.1	6.7	8
1973	4.1	2.9	1.2	0.1	8.3	11
1974	4.3	2.5	0.8	0.2	7.8	10
1975	3.3	1.4	0.6	0.1	5.4	7
1976	3.2	1.5	0.6	0.1	5.3	7
1977	4.7	2.3	0.9	0.1	8.0	10
1978	5.5	3.1	0.8	0.1	9.4	12
1979	6.0	3.8	0.8	0.1	10.6	13
1980	7.8	2.8	0.8	0.1	11.5	14
Total	45.9	24.6	7.8	0.9	79.1	100

Note: Numbers may not add to totals due to rounding.

Source: Standard and Poor's 1981b.

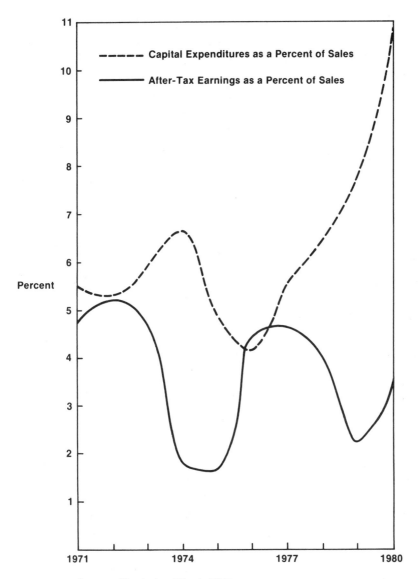

Source: Standard and Poor's 1981b

Figure 5.1
Comparison of Capital Expenditures and Earnings

between 1971 and 1980 were financed in the two worst years, 1974 and 1980. Furthermore, the internal sources of financing — retained earnings and depreciation — have accounted for over 60 percent of capital investments, even during the bad years (Table 5.3). In six out of the nine years shown in Table 5.3, internal sources met all the financing needs of the auto firms. The fact that the big four auto companies have managed to borrow $3.5 billion dollars as long-term debt in the worst year of the decade, 1980, is even more remarkable. Thus the assumption that the industry cannot finance its investments during bad times is without merit, at least on a historical basis.* The mere fact that all the auto firms have been able to introduce over half a dozen small, front-wheel drive automobiles suggests that financing has not been the constraining factor in their recovery. It is likely, however, that the industry may not be able to justify financing new investments in small-car plants without a significant improvement in the sales of these new models. In this sense, the firms do feel a capital constraint to the extent they are unable to persuade their stockholders of the merits of more plants.

BUSINESS TAX INCENTIVES

In the name of savings, investment, and job creation, the U.S. government has followed a policy of progressively increasing incentives for businesses. Whenever there has been a business recession and a sharp decline in the after-tax return on stockholder equity, the government has responded to public pressure with either an increased investment tax credit or an accelerated depreciation for tax purposes (Figure 5.2). The most recent subsidy scheme has been the "supply side" tax cuts,† which consist of new, liberal depreciation schedules and a provision for selling unused tax benefits. The net effect is often a negative effective tax rate on corporate income. For instance, because of a provision under which tax credits can be sold through a lease arrangement, General Motors managed to turn

---

*It is possible to argue that the auto firms have depleted their debt capacity with recent borrowings. It would be moot since the borrowing capacity is determined by the expectations of future performance, which again depends on new car sales as we argued earlier.

†The Economic Recovery Act of 1981.

TABLE 5.3
Major Sources of Funds for Capital Investment in the Auto Industry
(Million 1980 Dollars, Except Percentages)

| | Sources | | | | | Percentages | |
| | External | Internal | | | | | |
Year	Long-Term Debt Net Change	Retained Earnings	Depreciation	Total of Sources (Net of Debt Retirement)	Use in Capital Investment	Total Internal/Capital Investment	Long-Term Debt/Capital Investment
1972	730	3,360	6,240	10,330	6,730	140	11
1973	220	3,310	6,490	10,010	8,310	120	3
1974	1,140	150	5,090	6,390	7,760	70	15
1975	770	830	5,100	6,700	5,400	110	14
1976	−430	3,230	5,160	7,950	5,310	160	NM
1977	160	3,610	5,130	8,900	8,020	110	2
1978	−420	3,600	5,730	8,900	9,410	100	NM
1979	−220	2,350	5,800	7,930	10,640	80	NM
1980	3,510	0	6,660	10,170	11,450	60	31

NM = Not meaningful

Source: Standard and Poor's 1981b, data rounded.

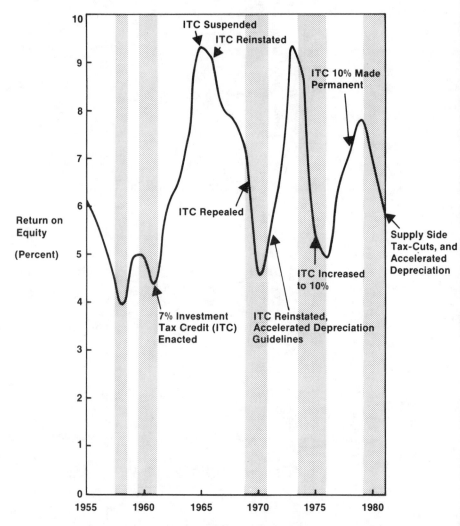

Return on Equity

(Percent)

ITC Suspended

ITC Reinstated

ITC 10% Made
Permanent

ITC Repealed

Supply Side
Tax-Cuts, and
Accelerated
Depreciation

7% Investment
Tax Credit (ITC)
Enacted

ITC Reinstated,
Accelerated Depreciation
Guidelines

ITC Increased
to 10%

Note: Return on equity is after-tax profits corrected for inflation effects
divided by current replacement cost of physical capital. The shaded areas
represent periods of business recessions.

Source: Council of Economic Advisors|1981|, p. 331

Figure 5.2
Historical Trend in After-Tax Rate
of Return on Stockholder's Equity
and Tax Incentives

their 1981 loss into a $333 million profit. Similarly, the new tax incentives have helped Chrysler and Ford post lower losses than they would otherwise have shown. Clearly, the improved performance of corporations such as General Motors, as indicated by their after-tax incomes, had very little to do with either the management competence or the improved sales of automobiles but a rather arbitrary change in tax laws.

It is true that tax incentives help capital formation, but they do not necessarily increase productivity nor create jobs as claimed by the advocates. For instance, the average capital invested per employee in the transportation equipment manufacturing sector has doubled between 1950 and 1976. Yet the growth rate in output per laborhour (productivity) has declined from over 5 percent per year in the 1950s to less than 1 percent per year during the late 1970s (U.S. Bureau of the Census 1981, pp. 414 and 560). Thus, tax incentives have merely intensified the use of capital in automobile production rather than do what they were originally intended for; that is, create jobs and increase productivity. Increased capital intensity may be necessary in the future to employ robotized production lines to improve quality and productivity. Capital alone cannot offset the effects of poor product design and costly labor and materials.

Even from a macroeconomic viewpoint tax incentives have not had their intended effects. While the aggregate savings rate has increased in the past three decades in response to investment incentives, the average growth rate in productivity (output per laborhour) has progressively declined (Figure 5.3). The case against tax incentives becomes even stronger when we compare the performance of six major industrial nations with comparably sized economies (Table 5.4). Japan and West Germany, with the lowest subsidy for capital recovery, rank relatively high on productivity growth and savings rate, while the United Kingdom and Canada, with the most liberal tax subsidies rank the lowest among the six countries. These facts suggest that increased investment incentives alone do not guarantee an increase in the growth rate of productivity. Yet tax subsidies have received undue emphasis in U.S. government policies.

What all this admittedly crude evidence points to is that U.S. corporations in general, and the automobile industry in particular, do not need new subsidies and tax incentives. Nothing short of salable products at competitive prices combined with an improved economy is likely to help the industry finance its new ventures.

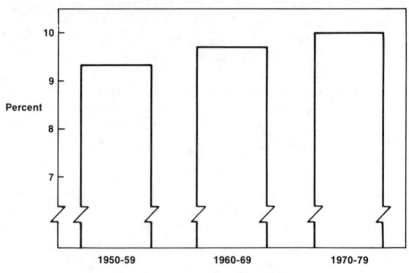

Non-Residential Fixed Investment as a Percent of GNP

Percent

10

9

8

7

| 1950-59 | 1960-69 | 1970-79 |

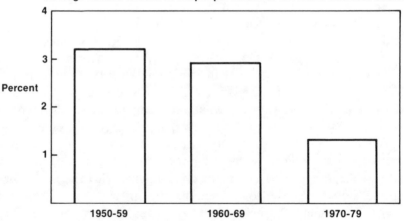

Average Annual Growth in Output per Manhour of Private Business Sector

Percent

4

3

2

1

| 1950-59 | 1960-69 | 1970-79 |

Source: Council of Economic Advisors 1980, pp. 247, 303

Figure 5.3
Ten Year Averages of Investment
Fraction and Labor Productivity Growth Rate

TABLE 5.4
Tax Incentives and Economic Performance
(Rankings of Selected Countries of Comparable Economies)

Country	Tax Incentives for Capital Investment[a]	Average Annual Growth Rate in Productivity[b] 1950-75	Average Savings Rate[c]
Japan	6	1	1
West Germany	5	3	2
France	4	4	3
Italy	3	2	6
Canada	2	5	4
United Kingdom	1	6	5

[a]The rankings were based on the average number of years for recovering 100 percent of capital investment. Japan ranked low with 11 years and the United Kingdom ranked high with 1 year; i.e., United Kingdom had the best tax incentives.

[b]Rankings based on Organization for Economic Cooperation and Development (OECD) statistics on output per manhour.

[c]Rankings based on nonresidential fixed business investment as a fraction of Gross Domestic Product, OECD statistics.

Sources: Ture and Sanden 1977, pp. 140-150; Organization for Economic Cooperation and Development 1980.

INDUSTRY SUBSIDIES AND OPPORTUNITY COSTS

By saving the Chrysler Corporation from bankruptcy with a $1.5 billion loan guarantee, the U.S. government has set a precedent and has conveniently avoided the important questions of economic efficiency. By assuming risk of default the government has committed tax revenues in a venture which was rejected as imprudent by the marketplace. There is no doubt that the automobile industry is important to the U.S. economy. It does not necessarily mean, though, that the auto industry should continue to remain important to our national economy at all costs. By guaranteeing $1.5 billion worth of Chrysler loans, the government has foregone the opportunity for guaranteeing the loans for retraining and relocating as many as 150,000 autoworkers (at $10,000 per person) who may have lost their jobs from a Chrysler bankruptcy. It is very likely that these individuals could be employed in more productive sectors of the U.S. economy. Similarly, a long list of missed opportunities can be drawn up and compared with the Chrysler loan guarantee to determine if it was the best choice in terms of economic efficiency.

The future of Chrysler remains cloudy, and there is still the risk of bankruptcy despite their new K-cars. The depressed economy is to be blamed for poor auto sales. That, however, calls for policies to improve the economy rather than subsidize investments.

In sum, the case for subsidizing new investments appears at best a weak one. The auto industry seems quite capable of financing large investments, and the reason for the current poor showing is the depressed sales of new models and the consequent lack of justification for new plants rather than the availability of capital. The industry has had adequate opportunity to create small automobiles competitive with the imports. The evidence so far suggests that the domestic automakers have a long road ahead.

6

The Management Solution

An important recent study suggests that over 60 percent of the $1400 landed cost advantage enjoyed by the Japanese for comparable automobiles is attributed to their superior management performance – particularly in management of inventories, product quality, and labor relations (Abernathy, Clark, and Kantrow 1981). This implies that more than anything else improved management techniques should help solve at least the short-term problems faced by domestic auto firms.

In this chapter we evaluate management performance specifically from the viewpoint of the stockholders. We also evaluate some of the recently suggested improvements in management techniques. We find that although improved management is necessary and can help, it is not likely to occur on its own without institutional changes in the basic corporate structure which ensure competent management. The automobile industry has eminently demonstrated that a handful of senior executives with significant influence over the allocation of 10 percent of our Gross National Output and 15 percent of our human resources can inflict severe damage to our economy by virtue of their incompetence. Thus it is in the legitimate interests of society to ensure superior management of its enterprises, particularly of the large, publicly held corporations.

Supposedly, the board of directors in the corporate structure is there to ensure that the managers are serving to maximize the wealth of the stockholders. In reality, however, the board is neither independent nor powerful enough to represent the stockholders' interest. Thus, we propose that an important reform is to make the board an independent, professional body which constantly monitors the performance of management, not only in terms of maximization of the tangible wealth of the stockholders but also the intangibles such as human wealth, consumer loyalty, and product plans. Such an arrangement is likely to improve the efficiency of our large enterprises and thus serve the larger interests of the society. The role of the board and its impact on the national economy and society at large is an important area of further research for management scientists and legal scholars. Here we can do no more justice than simply suggest certain directions for reform.

MANAGEMENT PERFORMANCE

There are two major criteria by which the performance of management can be judged. The first one is the rate of increase in the tangible wealth of stockholders relative to other investments of comparable risk. This is measured by the dividend yield and growth in the price of the stock. These are limited measures and provide little information about the future prospects of the firm. The future success of a firm depends largely on its ability to innovate and compete, which requires long-term plans that anticipate changes in market conditions. The market price of a firm's stock is generally assumed to reflect these attributes. In most market analyses of corporations one finds much emphasis on these factors.

Plans alone are insufficient to guarantee the sustained increase in stockholders' wealth. One of the important measures of the future performance of a firm is the degree of customer confidence and loyalty to its products and services, which depends to a large extent on the quality and reliability of the products. This is the intangible wealth of the stockholders. Short-sighted management can easily liquidate this important asset in its attempts to maximize short-term returns. Similar to customer loyalty, the commitment of employees to corporate goals is another important part of the intangible wealth. High turnover rates and poorly motivated employees can adversely affect the performance of a firm. Unfortunately, very little attention has been paid to these intangible components in measuring management performance. Auto industry managers have served their stockholders poorly on all counts. We shall specifically address these four areas of management performance: tangible wealth, product and process planning, consumer loyalty, and employee motivation.

Tangible Wealth

The primary responsibility of management is to increase the wealth of the stockholders, not merely for one or two years but for a sustained period. On the basis of this criterion the U.S. automakers performed, on the average, better than the market between 1950 and 1970 (White 1971, p. 248). It is not clear whether this performance derived from superior management or from simply being oligopolistic.

Had superior management been the principal reason for the above average performance, it is reasonable to expect it to have extended into the 1970s. But the auto industry performed poorly in the last decade as measured by total yield on stockholders' equity (from dividends and net appreciation). This yield was on the average less than the yield on a well-diversified investment portfolio made up of the Standard and Poor's 500 stocks (Table 6.1). Chrysler Corporation clearly emerges as the worst of the big four having managed to liquidate virtually the entire equity of its stockholders. Although General Motors, Ford, and American Motors have shown positive average returns for the past decade, they have done very poorly, even compared to the return on risk-free assets such as high grade bonds. Furthermore, if we factor in the average inflation rate of 7 percent for the decade (based on changes in GNP deflators) even General Motors, with the best performance record, has actually decreased the real wealth of its stockholders.

Product and Process Planning

One of the principal tasks of management is planning for the future to minimize the consequences of unexpected events. It requires development of a diversified product line to insure against rapid change in market conditions. Thus, planning requires taking into account the long lead times involved in changing production

TABLE 6.1
Average Annual Total Yield on Auto Stocks*
(Percent per Year)

Year	GM	Ford	Chrysler	AMC	Standard & Poor's 500	Moody's AAA Bond Yields
1971	21	40	14	−12	21	7
1972	1	15	23	17	14	7
1973	−9	−9	−10	−5	1	7
1974	−27	−24	−44	8	−18	9
1975	12	0	−19	−39	8	9
1976	59	41	51	6	22	8
1977	12	14	10	−25	1	8
1978	−4	8	−29	26	3	9
1979	5	−8	−20	31	13	10
1980	−9	−18	−12	−5	21	12
10 year average	6	6	−4	0	9	9

*Total yield is dividend plus stock appreciation.

Source: Value Line 1981; Council of Economic Advisors 1981, pp. 308 and 335.

lines to suit the market. It is precisely in this role that the U.S. auto firms have failed its stockholders. For instance, as early as 1973, following the oil embargo, there were signals that the supply of oil from the Middle East was uncertain. Between 1974 and the energy crisis of 1979, the U.S. automakers had five full years to design and perfect a small car that, in public perception, would be competitive with imports from Japan. Yet they have singularly failed in this task as indicated by a recent survey of car owners.

We compared a selected sample of domestic and Japanese cars for consumer attitudes using the *Consumer Reports* survey of owners (Figure 6.1). Of the models introduced between 1975 and 1980, the Japanese automobiles were rated consistently better than comparable U.S. automobiles in terms of both reliability and cost of operation.

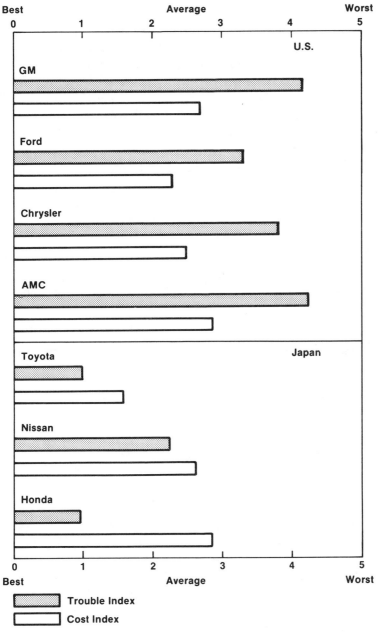

Best   Average   Worst

Source: Average index values over all small car models, 1975-1980 (Consumers Union 1981)

Figure 6.1
Trouble and Cost Indexes of
Domestic and Imported Japanese Cars

The safety recall data provide further evidence of poor management. For instance, between 1971 and 1980 domestic automobiles accounted for only 82 percent of the auto sales in the United States, but close to 95 percent of all cars recalled by the government for safety defects were made by domestic firms (Table 6.2). In comparison the top four imports made up of Toyota, Datsun, Honda, and Volkswagen were recalled proportionately less than their likely concentration in U.S. auto population.

It is easy to blame the autoworkers for the quality and reliability problems. But in a capital-intensive, assembly-line environment, workers have little control over the design, the manufacturing process, or the quality of parts from suppliers — factors that are clearly under management control.

Furthermore, recent studies attribute 40 percent of the landed cost advantage of Japanese imports to higher process yield (Abernathy, Clark, and Kantrow 1981, p. 76; U.S. Congress, House.

TABLE 6.2
Motor Vehicle Safety Recalls

	Number of Recalls			Number of Cars (Thousands)		
Year	Domestic	Imports	Percentage of Domestic	Domestic	Imports	Percentage of Domestic
1971	70	10	88	8,481	296	97
1972	83	6	93	2,458	373	87
1973	60	7	90	6,478	183	97
1974	66	8	89	2,194	162	93
1975	56	3	95	1,602	22	99
1976	60	3	95	2,855	44	99
1977	84	16	84	10,332	595	95
1978	91	18	83	7,671	223	97
1979	91	11	89	6,475	978	87
1980	41	19	89	3,047	500	86

Note: Domestics include models by GM, Ford, Chrysler, and AMC, which accounted for 82 percent of all cars sold betweeen 1971 and 1980. Imports include Toyota, Datsun, Honda, and VW, which accounted for 12 percent of all cars sold between 1971 and 1980.

Source: U.S. Department of Transportation 1971-80.

Committee on Banking, Finance, and Urban Affairs 1981b, testimony by J. Harbour). These studies note low work-in-process inventories and a cooperative system of defect prevention *by workers* as being the prime factors in achieving high process yield. This is a direct indictment of U.S. managers for poor design of the manufacturing process.

Consumer Loyalty

The third measure of management performance is consumer loyalty. Consumers today are far more sophisticated and organized than they were even a decade ago, especially when it comes to large expenditures for durable goods. The influence of consumer interest groups has intensified the competition faced by domestic automakers. Now, not only do consumers face a large number of small car manufacturers, but also organizations which thrive in comparative ratings of products. The power of consumer service organizations is exemplified by the fact that when *Consumers Report* magazine rated the new 1978 Dodge Omni and Plymouth Horizon as being "unacceptable," the news made headlines and sales quickly dropped. Chrysler Corporation had to modify the automobile in order to allay consumer fears over the stability of these two models at highway speeds.

A recent survey of car buyers conducted by General Motors shows that consumers perceive the condition of new foreign cars at delivery to be much superior to that of domestic cars (*Washington Post* 1981, p. G-1). Another survey by J. D. Power and Associates suggests that compared to Japanese cars, U.S. cars are perceived by consumers to be declining in quality of workmanship, design, value, and dependability (Figure 6.2). As a consequence, domestic cars attract only 78 percent repeat customers on the average compared to 91 percent for imports (Abernathy, Clark, and Kantrow 1981, p. 75). It may take years for domestic auto companies to regain consumer loyalty to the extent that existed in prior decades.

Employee Motivation

Poor products also result from poorly motivated employees. A major indicator of motivation problems is absenteeism rates. Abernathy rates absenteeism as the third most significant factor after

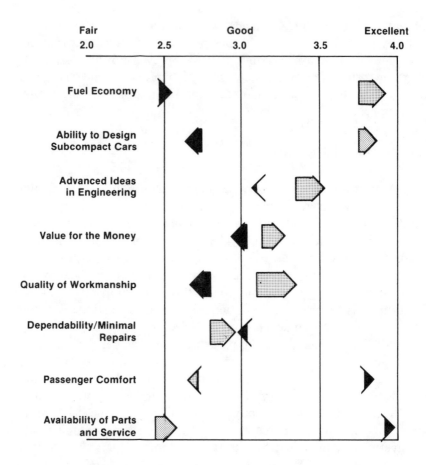

Note: Base of each arrow represents the mean scores received on each item from a Consumer Survey in June 1979 and the tips represent the mean scores received on the same items from a February 1981 survey. All arrows pointing to the right represent an increase in mean score and all arrows pointing to the left, a decrease. Finally, the length of the arrows illustrate the amount of change.

Source: J.D. Power and Associates 1981

Figure 6.2
A Comparison of Consumer Perceptions
of Domestic and Imported Japanese Cars

manufacturing process and job structure in determining the cost advantage enjoyed by the Japanese automakers (Abernathy, Clark, and Kantrow 1981, p. 76). Although reliable statistics are not available, there seems to be a general concurrence that unexcused absences are higher among the U.S. workers. James Harbour (1981), a leading expert on U.S. and Japanese auto industry, reports that an average U.S. worker is absent without excuse 8 percent of his work time compared to only 2 percent for Japanese workers. Decline in motivation leads to the steady erosion of human capital assets of the firm which will sooner or later reflect in the financial performance of the firm. Thus, the U.S. auto managers must again be judged as poor performers based on this last of the four criteria we have considered so far.

A critique of past performance of management would be incomplete without suggestions for improvement. Many suggestions have already been made by various experts. In the rest of this chapter we shall consider some of the managerial solutions to the near-term problems faced by the auto industry.

MANAGEMENT REMEDIES

The recent emergence of Japanese automakers as leading in the world has made them a standard of comparison of managerial performance; they are worthy of emulation. Three specific areas of Japanese management have received much attention in the United States recently. These are inventory control, quality control, and labor relations. We shall consider each of these three areas to see if it would be to the advantage of U.S. auto firms to follow the Japanese methods.

Inventory Control

The Japanese auto firms follow a concept of "just-in-time" inventory system by which their work-in-process inventories are kept between two hours and two days of requirement in the assembly line. In contrast, it has been estimated that the U.S. manufacturers keep a 10-day minimum level (*Automotive News*, December 21, 1981). The "just-in-time" approach clearly reduces the need for financing large inventories and consequently reduces the holding costs of assembly operation. Should then the U.S. companies follow this system? The answer cannot be an unqualified yes. The optimal size of inventories is always a matter of tradeoff between time lost in production (or lost sales) and holding costs. As a rule the larger the uncertainty in either the demand for cars or the supply of quality components, the higher will be the level of inventories for given storage and financing costs (which is again determined by the opportunity cost for the firm). Part of the reason why the Japanese can work with a small level of inventory is that during the past decade the demand for Japanese cars has grown steadily without any serious fluctuations. In contrast the U.S. automakers have been subjected to swings in consumer demand (Figure 6.3). Another reason for generally larger inventories carried by domestic automakers is their historic market position. As giant oligopolies, they have come to depend on a network of plants and suppliers who are widely dispersed geographically. This dispersion of production units requires a long pipeline of parts, which merely adds to the inventory costs. Thus, what is an optimal level of inventories for the Japanese may not necessarily be optimal for U.S. manufacturers. Nonetheless, competitive pressures require that future inventory costs per automobile be reduced drastically. In order to achieve this, the U.S. network of auto plants and supplier facilities may require considerable restructuring.

Quality Control

As a consequence of the "just-in-time" inventory system it becomes necessary in Japan to delegate much of the quality control responsibility to the workers on the assembly line. There is very little time for a thorough examination by a separate battery of workers. Abernathy states that " . . . the (just-in-time) system will not work if frequent or lengthy breakdowns occur, it creates inescapable pressure for maximizing uptime and minimizing defects." (Abernathy, Clark, and Kantrow 1981, p. 75). The Japanese worker enjoys much autonomy on the line and can stop the entire production line in case of defective parts.

To some extent the Japanese system works because of a characteristic loyalty of employees and suppliers and a general commitment. It is interesting, however, to note that the Japanese products

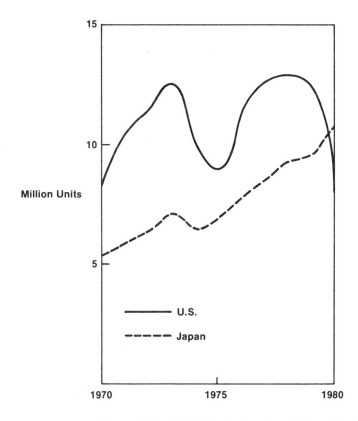

Source: Motor Vehicle Manufacturers Association, various issues

Figure 6.3
U.S. and Japanese Motor Vehicle Production

were notorious for their shoddiness as recently as 15 years ago, even though they had the benefit of highly motivated managers, workers, and suppliers. Thus, it is difficult to attribute any one single factor as being the primary reason for the now superior quality of Japanese products. It could either be interpreted as a transient phenomena which may change as rising affluence changes the attitudes of employees toward work and leisure, or as a truly remarkable achievement from which we can learn. The Japanese system of quality control may not necessarily work in the United States. Rather, a system of incentives for individuals or small groups or some other form of group motivation may work better. As demonstrated by

Volkswagen of America, U.S. workers are quite capable of producing a quality product under good management.

Improved Labor Relationships

In the past few years, the large Japanese firms have become a standard against which U.S. firms have been compared in the area of labor relationships. Two recent studies (Ouchi 1981; Pascale and Athos 1981) advocate adopting Japanese ideas of management, especially in the area of labor relations. The art of Japanese management consists of minimizing conflict and earning the trust and commitment of workers.

Conflict is an ubiquitous force in U.S. labor-management relationships. The adversarial relationship is wasteful of resources; historically, the U.S. auto industry has been able to accommodate it mainly due to its oligopolistic power. The autoworkers are paid higher than other comparatively skilled manufacturing workers. The current competition has, however, forced U.S. auto industry labor and management to minimize conflict as their very survival is being threatened. The recent concessions by the United Auto Workers and the management at Ford and Chrysler mark the beginning of a new and more hopeful era for U.S. industrial relations. No longer are stockholders' interests in conflict with those of labor.

Temporary wage concessions are not, however, indicative of any fundamental change in labor-management relations. Historically, management of people has proven to be the most difficult task for U.S. corporations. The famous Hawthorne experiment and pioneering work done by MacGregor (1960), Maslow (1954), and Argyris (1964) have helped us understand the complexity of the problem more than they have offered any solutions. It is very likely, for instance, the inventory control problems will be solved by U.S. managers in a relatively short time compared to the difficulties they are bound to face in managing the human resources. Pascale and Athos state that,

> Today's world competition poses an organizational challenge that cannot be met simply by technology or financial resources. Technological innovations and resource allocation are outcomes of human processes. Our success is not inevitable. Our ability to compete rests on our ability to organize human beings in such a way as to generate

opportunity and results, rather than impasses, stagnation, bureaucracy, and wasteful friction. (Pascale and Athos 1981, p. 33).

The remedy suggested by these authors is that "we must change the way we think," and learn from the Japanese about human resource management. Although some corporations have been successful, adopting the views of another culture may prove difficult, if not impossible, especially for the managers of automobile firms. We may need more than an appeal for change in the ways of thinking. We may need institutional reform.

THE NEED FOR INSTITUTIONAL REFORM

The mere fact that a handful of senior automobile executives can adversely affect the lives of hundreds and thousands of workers, stockholders, banks, and even local and state governments is indicative of the need for competent managers. An institution that is supposed to ensure managerial competence is a corporate board of directors, which supposedly represents the legitimate interests of the stockholders. Peter Drucker (1974, p. 28) the noted expert on management, suggests that "The board, whatever its name and whatever its legal structure, has become a fiction." Drucker warns that without a strong board to evaluate and control management, society would sooner or later intervene and impose its will through politically appointed members as in Sweden and West Germany (Drucker 1974, p. 630).

The role of a board of directors should be defined more broadly than it is now. For instance, its current duties call for representing the stockholders' interests by exercising partial control over the allocative powers of managers. The source of a board's authority lies in its power to hire and fire managers, but very rarely does one hear of a top manager being fired by a board for low consumer loyalty, poor morale among employees, or inadequate product plans. The automobile industry is an excellent case in point, where the same managers continue to operate year after year despite a poor showing. Even when someone is discharged for reasons other than profit performance, he is quickly recycled into the industry. As a result, despite the availability of the best technology, brain power, and one of the most productive of workforces in the world, the U.S. managers have failed to deal effectively with the new international competition.

It is generally held that during times of rapidly changing market conditions, old capital goods become obsolete and must be rapidly replaced to remain competitive. In the case of the auto industry, the old assembly lines must be converted rapidly to produce small cars. This is likewise true for human capital as it is embodied in the management. Managers who have come up through the ranks in an era of little competition and cosmetic innovations may be poorly equipped to cope with the new market conditions; they may continue to operate under old assumptions which are no longer valid. In this case it is in the best interests of the stockholders to hire a new team in order to meet the new challenge. Currently, however, there is very little recourse for the stockholders against incompetent management except to move their holdings from one firm to another. If a sufficient number of people follow suit, then presumably the firm will go out of business.

In real life it rarely works out as elegantly as the free-market theory would suggest, but rather the firms, particularly the large ones, continue to operate with the same management. Even when stockholders abandon the firm, management often turns to government for subsidies as in the case of Chrysler or for trade restrictions as in the case of Ford Motor Company. If political lobbying provides a higher return than research and development, it is only logical to expect rational managers to pursue that course. The nation would be poorer for this.

In addition, inordinate amounts of management time and effort go into preparing the generally useless, platitudinous corporate annual reports for stockholder's consumption. It would be a very beneficial instrument if it contained even half the legally required information reported to the Securities and Exchange Commission in the 10-K forms. Ideally, the board of directors should report on the management performance, future prospects, and potential problems in a detached manner so that a stockholder can benefit from the information. Examples of relevant information include: consumer surveys, product ratings, long-term plans, and employee turnover rates.

Finally, for the board to be effective, as Peter Drucker suggests, it should consist of full time, professional members who are independent of corporate management, its bankers, and its suppliers. The members should be elected to a single term. Without this, the board will remain merely a cosmetic body with no powers. Reform of this magnitude, however, requires changes in laws, which may ultimately lead to efficient and competitive enterprises that would benefit our nation.

7

The Need for Regulatory Reform

The automobile is one of the most heavily regulated products in the United States. Although there may be some justification for the past regulations, there is an urgent need to reevaluate the entire basis of safety, environmental, and fuel-efficiency regulations. In this chapter we argue that even though the recent proposals by the Reagan Administration will be of some help to the automobile industry, there needs to be a much more sweeping reform of auto regulations, particularly in light of the competitiveness of the current marketplace.

THE REGULATORY BURDEN AND RECENT RELIEF

Government regulation of business is often criticized by corporate executives as being costly and burdensome — especially during times of economic downturns and depressed sales. This is particularly true in the case of the automobile industry which in recent years has faced a large number of product regulations. The industry's attitude toward government regulation is reflected in statements made by Dr. David S. Potter, a Group Vice President for Public Affairs with the General Motors Corporation. In his testimony at recent U.S. Senate hearings on auto industry regulations, he stated that:

Excessive regulation is sapping manpower and profits at a time when they are desperately needed to help restore the industry to health, and meet the stiff competition from abroad. Should anyone doubt the magnitude of the situation, I would point out that in the six-year period 1974 to 1979, General Motors spent more than $8 billion complying with all regulations. In 1979 alone, the cost was nearly $2 billion and required the equivalent effort of 26,000 full time employees. (Auto Hearings 1981, p. 21)

This statement suggests that in 1979, General Motors' corporate expenditures for complying with regulations were over 40 percent of their capital expenditures. Thus, it would appear that even a partial deregulation would free substantial capital and manpower which could be used to counter the competition from abroad.

Following the industry's viewpoint the Reagan Administration implemented a set of programs to help the automobile industry through regulatory reform and economic recovery (White House 1981). The administration hopes to achieve lower inflation, lower interest rates, increased investment, and economic growth from both tax cuts and a balanced budget. In the area of regulatory reform, the administration proposed a set of actions in 1981 to eliminate or slow down the schedule of new safety and environmental standards affecting passenger cars. The administration estimated that over the next five years, the savings from this partial deregulation will be $1 billion for manufacturers and $8 billion for consumers (without any discounting of the benefit stream). This amounts to about $160 per car (Table 7.1). Since these estimates were published in April 1981, the National Highway Traffic Safety Administration (NHTSA) has rescinded the passive restraint standard.* General Motors estimates that this would increase the industry's capital savings to $1.4 billion and consumer savings to over $10 billion (Auto Hearings 1981, p. 30). The average savings per car over the five-year period, 1981-85 would be $210.

Is the proposed regulatory reform policy likely to help the domestic auto industry significantly? An analysis of the proposed administration actions by *Automotive News* (April 27, 1981, p. 2)

---

*It should be noted that although the mandatory passive restraint standard was canceled, much controversy remains. It is very likely that there will be continued pressure from consumer protection groups and insurance industry representatives to reinstate the standard.

TABLE 7.1
Reagan Administration Proposals to Deregulate
the Passenger Car Sector

Proposed Action	Five-Year Savings (Million 1981 Dollars Undiscounted Five-Year Totals)	
	Capital Savings for Industry	*Savings for Consumers*
Environmental Standards		
Emissions averaging for diesel particulates.	40	523
Eliminate 1984 high altitude emissions standards and adopt self-certification for vehicles sold at high altitudes.	39	1301
Do not require use of onboard control technology for refueling emissions.	103	1200
Reduce the annual number of assembly line test orders and defer standards for paint shops.	301	1
Safety Standards		
Delay 1982 implementation of passive-restraint standard for large cars.	30	105
Modify the bumper standards.	—	3250
Rescind the fields of direct view standard.	174	85
Other actions.	-352	1540
Total savings	*1039*	*8005*

Note: Assuming 10 million units per year of sales, the consumer savings amounts to $160 per car.

Source: White House 1981, page A-60. (Table does not include proposed actions directed toward trucks.)

suggests that they will help most those who need help least. The analysis indicates that General Motors, with a diversified product line, and the Japanese automakers will be the primary beneficiaries of deregulation. For example, the Environmental Protection Agency's (EPA) proposed modification of the 1984 standard for particulate emissions from diesel engines will benefit those companies that manufacture diesel engines — General Motors, Volkswagen, and the importers. Also General Motors and the Japanese automakers are in much better financial positions than either Ford, Chrysler, or AMC; yet the savings from deregulation would benefit them more.

All of the proposed deregulatory actions except one relate to cars. (The one exception is the standard on hydrocarbon emissions from manufacturing plants — primarily paint facilities.) Thus, the proposed administration actions will provide only marginal relief from foreign competition, as they will help foreign car makers almost as much as the domestic industry. In addition the estimated savings of $1.4 billion in capital investment over the next five years is only about 3 percent (U.S. Department of Transportation 1981a, p. 64) of the estimate of $50 billion needed for rebuilding the industry. Thus, unless the $210 reduction in car price increases sales substantially, the proposed actions will not significantly affect the industry.

Both the price reduction that would result from regulatory reform and the President's economic recovery program, assuming it will work, should improve sales. At an average selling price of $9000 per car, the $210 price reduction from deregulation is 2.3 percent of the retail price. This would increase sales by about 250,000 units per year from the current level of 6 million units, under an optimistic assumption of a −1.8 price elasticity of demand.* In addition, it is quite likely, given the current trends, that 25 to 30 percent of the increase in sales will be captured by imported cars.

In contrast, if the administration's tax policies help reduce inflation and, consequently, the interest rates, they are likely to help passenger car sales more than regulatory reform. For instance, a mere 2 percent drop in the current interest rate for new car financing could increase car sales by as much as all the deregulation policies. The reduction of interest rates from 16 to 14 percent on a three-year loan of $7000 will save $400 in finance charges. On a present value basis this is equivalent to $300 off the purchase price — greater than the reduction achieved by deregulation. Similarly, if the administration's economic policies help increase the real growth of the median family income by for example, 2 percent per year, then assuming a pessimistic value of 2.0 for income elasticity, the increase

---

*In a recent Oakridge National Laboratory study, David Greene (1981, p. 2.61) summarized estimates of short-run price elasticities of demand which ranged betweeen −1.8 and −0.3.

in auto sales would be greater than from the cost reduction due to deregulation.

Although the proposed remedies of the Reagan administration will provide some help to the auto industry, they do not fully address the inconsistencies between many of the regulatory goals and the enacted regulations. Even though there is some justification for past industry regulation, there seems to be very little rationale for continued regulation. In the following section we shall consider the regulatory goals and suggest alternative approaches to regulation in the areas of safety, emission control, fuel-economy standards, and in work-place regulations.

REGULATORY GOALS

Historically, regulations have been imposed on industries as a result of public outcries against unsafe products, unsafe working conditions, and resultant dirty environment. Generally, they have been based on reactions against business negligence rather than on any rational plan. Usually the goals of health and safety regulations have been to save people from avoidable injuries and premature deaths. For instance, the principal goal of automobile safety regulations has been to minimize the 50,000 lives lost annually on our roads and highways, to reduce the estimated 2 million cases of serious injuries, and to save some of the $50 billion in property damages (U.S. Department of Transportation 1980, p. 1). Public demand for a cleaner environment made it necessary to reduce emissions from the internal combustion engine. In addition, the 1973 oil embargo and the subsequent quadrupling of imported-oil prices necessitated energy conservation to reduce our vulnerability to foreign oil supplies. One of the best ways for implementing conservation was to improve the fuel efficiency of automobiles that account for 60 percent of the imported oil consumed in this country.

Saving lives, improving the quality of air, and reducing our dependence on imported oil were the original goals for which regulations were proposed. Although there is a general public concurrence on these goals, much debate exists on the means of accomplishing them. For instance, some argue that regulation of the auto industry is not necessarily the most efficient way to accomplish these goals. Economic theory offers some guidance in the selection of efficient policies for achieving social goals (See Henderson and Quandt 1971, Ch. 7. for an introduction to this subject).

Economic theory suggests that the normal market mechanism, though efficient in allocating resources between competing ends, frequently fails to provide socially desirable goods such as clean air and water. The failure of markets is generally attributed to the presence of monopolies and what are known as "externalities." Externalities are spillover effects from private sector activities: pollution caused by automobile exhausts or highway traffic noise. In these cases the cost of the externalities, imposed on the public by users of automobiles, are not fully borne by those who benefit from automobiles. Since in a complex society such as ours these problems cannot be solved through direct negotiations between affected parties, government must intervene and impose fines, taxes, user fees, rules, and regulations. The problem becomes simple if everyone has identical preferences on safety and environment. We live in a pluralistic society, however, where different individuals value clean air, water, and human life differently. Thus, what may be optimal and elegant solutions on paper may seem as crude compromises to different interest groups in society. Furthermore, much controversy remains as to the very notion of "externality" (See, for instance, Dahlman 1979).

Therefore, lacking a solid theoretical basis, we must tentatively accept a weaker premise; cleaner air and water and safer automobiles are equally preferred by everyone. The problem then is to find the most efficient method of achieving these social goals. Federal regulation is only one of the alternatives by which these goals can be obtained. A review of the history of auto industry regulations, however, suggests that the U.S. Congress has preferred the regulatory approach without much regard for cost effectiveness. This may be partly due to the fact that cost effectiveness may not have been a relevant criterion in achieving socially desirable ends. Rather, from a legislator's viewpoint, achieving social objectives by coercing (regulating) the least number of voters may have been a much stronger motivation than economic efficiency. Analysis of individual areas of automotive regulations in the following sections seems to lend support to the theory that political expediency preempts economic efficiency in regulatory decisions.

SAFETY REGULATIONS

Under increasing political pressure, the auto companies began introducing safety features in the early 1960s (White 1971). By 1964 seat belts were standard equipment on all cars. In the same year Congress directed the General Services Administration to issue safety standards for cars purchased by the federal government.

In 1966, amid public demand for safety led by consumer activist Ralph Nader, Congress passed the National Traffic and Motor Vehicle Safety Act and created the National Highway Traffic Safety Administration (NHTSA). NHTSA was empowered to issue safety-related product recalls and to set standards for improving the safety of the automobile. The rationale for safety regulations at the time was that U.S. auto industry, dominated by General Motors, was monopolistic, as it faced very little competition in the large car market (Nash 1981, p. 64). Careful analysis of the industry structure at the time has supported this claim (White 1975).

Traffic safety depends on the design and condition of the automobile, the condition of the roads and highways, and on the drivers. The Federal Highway Administration has done much to improve the roads and highways, and NHTSA has imposed over 50 safety standards which relate to the design and performance of automobiles. The intent of these standards has been to help the occupants of automobiles avoid severe injuries or death in case of accidents. The standards specifically relate to windshield resistance, the energy absorption by steering columns, interior padding, side-marker lights, theft protection, side-door strength, and seat and shoulder belts. NHTSA claims that " . . . safety regulations have been a major factor in the decline of the fatality rate over the last decade . . . (and that) its safety standards have saved more than 55,000 lives through 1978, a number that is increasing by nearly 10,000 per year as newer, safer vehicles replace older, less safe ones." (U.S. Department of Transportation 1979a, p. iii).

First let us review NHTSA's claims. In Table 7.2 the highway fatality rate data for selected periods are shown. The fatality rate per 100 million vehicle miles of travel declined between 1950 and 1960 at an average annual rate of 3.6 percent even though there were no safety regulations. However, it started to rise between 1960 and

TABLE 7.2
Motor Vehicle Traffic Fatalities

Year	Total Deaths	Per 10,000 Motor Vehicles	Per 100 Million Vehicle Miles	Percent Decrease From Previous Year[c]
1940	34,500	10.63	11.42	—
1950	34,800	7.07	7.59	4.0
1960	38,100	5.12	5.31	3.5
1966[a]	53,000	5.53	5.70	−1.2
1970	54,600	4.92	4.88	3.8
1971	54,400	4.68	4.57	6.4
1972	56,300	4.60	4.43	3.1
1973	55,500	4.28	4.24	4.3
1974[b]	46,400	3.44	3.59	15.3
1975	45,900	3.33	3.45	3.9
1976	47,000	3.28	3.34	3.2
1977	49,500	3.33	3.35	−0.3
1978	51,500	3.41	3.39	−1.2
1979	52,800	3.30	3.45	−1.5
1980	53,300	3.23	3.53	−2.3

[a]The National Highway Transportation Safety Administration was created in 1966.

[b]55 MPH speed limit on highways was implemented in 1974.

[c]Decrease in deaths per year per 100 million vehicle miles averaged over prior interval.

Source: Motor Vehicle Manufacturers Association 1981, p. 50.

1966 at over 1 percent per year. Soon after NHTSA was created in 1966 and safety standards were implemented, there was a sudden reversal in the fatality rate trend. The fatality rate declined at an annual average rate of 4.3 percent between 1966 and 1973, which gives partial credence to the claims made by NHTSA.

Then, as an energy conservation measure following the OPEC oil embargo, the highway speed limits were lowered in 1974 from 65 miles per hour (in some places from 75 mph) to 55 mph. The fatality rate subsequently dropped dramatically by a record 18 percent in the first year. Since then, however, the rate has remained relatively constant at about 3.5 deaths per 100 million vehicle miles, despite the fact that most of NHTSA's standards were in full effect during this period.

Using NHTSA's logic in determining the number of lives saved, it appears that the oil embargo and the subsequent lowering of speed limits has saved almost 100,000 lives in the last seven years. This raises the possibility that more lives would have been saved had the highway speed limit been lowered to 55 mph in 1966 than were saved by safety standards. However, it is possible that the enforcement costs would have been prohibitive in 1966, because the public would have been far less receptive to lower speed limits than they were after the oil embargo. Nonetheless, the speed limit alternative was not given serious consideration as a safety issue. Even when it was implemented in 1974 it was sold on the ground of energy conservation rather than safety.

In sum, although there is some justification for past regulations on the design of automobiles, additional regulations on design appear to be unwarranted. Moreover, improved designs and safer roads only partially address the issue of traffic safety. Proper maintenance of vehicles and the condition of drivers need far more attention than they have received in the past. The case for continued product regulation is made even weaker by the fact that 70 percent of the fatal accidents result from improper driving such as speeding, disregarding signs and signals, and driving left of center. In addition, over 75 percent of traffic injuries are attributed to improper driving (National Safety Council 1981, p. 48). NHTSA's own studies (U.S. Department of Transportation 1978) indicate that nearly 50 percent of all the fatally injured drivers were legally drunk. In four studies conducted in four states, the data show that 40 to 55 percent of all fatally injured drivers had a blood alcohol concentration (BAC) of .10 percent w/v* or more (Figure 7.1). These drivers were too intoxicated to drive legally in most states. The NHTSA study further reports that there was a high involvement of drivers with drinking problems and, more importantly, with a history of prior arrests for drunk driving.

Thus, traffic fatalities are, to a large extent, externalities imposed by an identifiable group of individuals on the rest of society — that is, individuals who drive under the influence of alcohol and disregard traffic regulations. Therefore, the rational approach would dictate that this group should be sufficiently penalized and discouraged from

---

*A BAC of .10 percent w/v means that there is .10 grams (weight) of alcohol in a 100 milliliter (volume) sample of blood.

Fatally Injured Drivers with BACs in Given Ranges

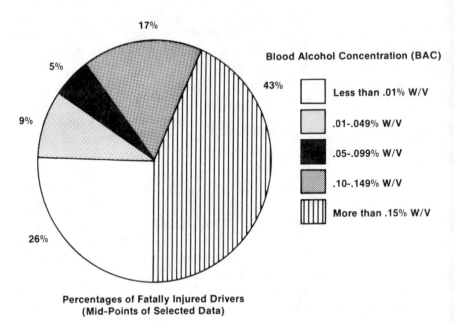

Percentages of Fatally Injured Drivers
(Mid-Points of Selected Data)

Fatally Injured Drivers with BACs Exceeding Given Amounts

BAC	Percentage of Fatally Injured Drivers	
	Range	Mid-Point of Range
.15% W/V or more	34-53	43
.10% W/V or more	55-65	60
.05% W/V or more	60-70	65

Data from California, Vermont, Michigan and New York, 1958-1969. The W/V units refer to weight of alcohol per volume of blood.

Source: U.S. Department of Transportation 1978, p. 9

Figure 7.1
Blood Alcohol Concentrations of Drivers Killed
in Single-Vehicle, Non-Pedestrian Crashes

imposing undue costs on society. Although there is some effort by the current administration in developing better programs to fight drunk driving, the direction of the government's efforts has been to regulate the automobile industry to design safer cars rather than to impose adequate constraints or penalties on the responsible group of individuals. Unfortunately, insurance firms, which are also subject to regulations, have failed to provide a market solution to the problems arising from irresponsible drivers. Rather, the industry has become an advocate of vehicle safety regulations, and has been lobbying against the auto industry in favor of passive restraints (Auto Hearing 1981, p. 76).

The passive-restraint case provides a clear example of the need to consider alternatives to regulation. This standard requires that vehicle occupants be protected in a 30 mph crash against a fixed barrier. At the present time there are only two alternatives which will satisfy this performance standard. One is the automatic safety belt, and the other is the air bag which inflates during accidents and cushions the vehicle's occupants. In 1977, the Secretary of Transportation issued a requirement that passive restraints be available in all full-sized cars in model year 1982, intermediates and compacts in model year 1983, and for all cars in model year 1984. This is known as Federal Motor Vehicle Safety Standard 208.

In April 1981, the NHTSA delayed implementation of the standard for one year and agreed to continue reviewing the regulation (White House 1981, p. A-34). In October 1981, the agency announced that they were rescinding the passive-restraint standard entirely. This decision was based partly on the fact that the auto industry had halted air-bag development and had planned to comply with the regulation by installing automatic, passive-belt systems.

By NHTSA's own account this is one of the most thoroughly evaluated standards in the history of the agency (Nash 1981, p. 57). NHTSA estimates that this standard would save about 9000 lives each year. The full savings would not be achieved until ten years after the regulation began when all cars were equipped (U.S. Department of Transportation 1980, p. 4). The standard is generally defended on the grounds that less than 12 percent of car drivers use the seat belts that are currently available in all cars. Moreover, two recent surveys suggest that there is popular support for the safety standard. One was conducted by the Opinion Research Corporation for NHTSA (U.S. Department of Transportation 1980,

p. 39). This survey indicated that conventional automatic seat belts were used 80 percent of the time compared to conventional seat and shoulder belts which were used less than 12 percent of the time. The second survey, conducted by General Motors, indicated that 70 percent of the drivers sampled responded favorably to the air-cushion restraint system even at a cost of $360 per car (U.S. Department of Transportation 1980, p. 10). Passive restraint standards then must be justified on the grounds that since consumers may not voluntarily choose to use conventional seat belts, they may be induced into purchasing passive restraints if offered at a reasonable cost. The best way to achieve low costs is to mass produce the passive-restraint systems and have them installed in the automobiles during assembly. One possible way to achieve this is through regulation, but there are other alternatives.

One alternative is to observe if consumers will really demand passive restraints as the surveys indicate. In today's competitive market it is likely that there will be attempts to market safety as an additional feature. A second method is to view the problem in terms of positive social benefits. The benefits to society from implementing the passive-restraint standard far exceed the benefit to any single individual. For instance, Professor William Nordhaus of Yale University estimates that the implementation of Federal Motor Vehicle Safety Standard 208 will cost $1.1 billion (Auto Hearings 1981, p. 106) while the benefits to society in terms of lives saved and injuries avoided will amount to $11 billion. This is a social benefit to cost ratio of ten to one, an impressive social rate of return. In comparison, Nordhaus estimates only a three to one benefit to cost ratio for an individual consumer. Thus, it would pay society to subsidize the implementation of the safety standard entirely, at least for a few years or until the industry recovers fully. An equitable way to accomplish this is to use the revenues from federal excise taxes on tires and gasoline so that those who use automobiles will pay for the cost of the subsidized safety. A third possibility is for the insurance industry to subsidize implementation of the standard from the revenues it could collect as special premiums for irresponsible driving. This would impose more of the cost on those most likely to benefit.

Another alternative would be to attempt a stepwise implementation plan. Rather than impose the regulation on the entire nation, first have selected states adopt the regulation. This would insure sufficient volume to achieve mass-produced costs, and the experience could be used to resolve some of the questions of effectiveness consumer acceptance. If after a few years of experience, the passive restraints were found to be as effective as proponents claim, then there would be demand for them from consumers in other states. States could be encouraged to participate through a modest federal subsidy program and with the help of model legislation. States with high fatality rates would be inclined to adopt the regulation, and passive restraints would not necessarily be forced on individuals who live in low fatality areas such as Washington, D.C., and Rhode Island.

Finally, the government could initiate a massive public education campaign to encourage passenger car occupants to use the existing lap and shoulder belts. It has been estimated that if all occupants used safety belts at least 12,000 lives would be saved annually (National Safety Council 1981, p. 53). These savings would begin immediately and at no direct cost to the auto consumer or the industry. In contrast, passive-restraint regulations would require ten years before the full potential of 9,000 lives saved annually could be achieved at a considerable cost to both consumer and industry. Of course, an education campaign could not expect to be totally effective. Even if the usage rate was doubled from the current 12 percent to 24 percent, over 1,600 lives would be saved annually. Furthermore, an education campaign would have additional benefits. It would increase public awareness of the potential dangers of driving and thereby encourage safer driving. Furthermore, such a campaign might shift people's perception of the responsibility for personal safety from the federal government and the auto industry back to the individual.

At present there is an urgent need to study these and other possible alternatives to improving auto safety. It is also worthwhile to investigate whether we have reached diminishing returns from design modifications and whether national resources will be better spent in enforcing proper maintenance and operation of automobiles.

ENVIRONMENTAL REGULATIONS

Just as safety regulations, environmental regulations have had a significant impact on the automobile industry. Following the initiative of the state of California, the U.S. Congress passed the Motor Vehicle Air Pollution Act of 1965. In accordance with the Act, the Secretary of Health, Education, and Welfare set exhaust standards, effective January 1, 1968, which would cut hydrocarbons 25 percent and carbon monoxide 40 percent. (For more details, see White 1977.) In 1969, Congress passed the National Environmental Policy Act and established the Environmental Protection Agency (EPA). Through amendments to the Clean Air Act in 1970 and 1977, Congress mandated that automobile exhaust emissions of hydrocarbons and carbon monoxide be reduced by 95 percent and emissions of nitrogen oxides by 75 percent from uncontrolled levels. In Table 7.3 the standards and their schedule of implementation are shown.

Currently, there is a debate in Congress over freezing the standards at the 1980 levels (*Automotive News*, September 28, 1981). The recent hearings centered on the issue of rolling tailpipe emissions back to 1980 levels of seven grams per mile for carbon dioxide and two grams per mile for nitrogen oxides. This is in spite of the fact that almost all new 1981 and 1982 cars meet the 1981 standard. This debate will continue well into 1982.

There is little doubt that regulation has had a positive effect on the levels of pollutants emitted by motor vehicles. Figure 7.2 shows the dramatic reduction in emissions of carbon monoxide, hydrocarbons, and nitrogen oxide that followed the implementation of

TABLE 7.3
Motor Vehicle Emissions Standards
(Grams per Mile)

	Hydrocarbons	Carbon Monoxide	Nitrogen Oxides
Uncontrolled cars	8.70	87.0	4.0
Original limits for 1975-76	0.41	3.4	0.4
Actual new car limits for			
1968-69	5.90	50.8	*
1970-71	3.90	33.3	*
1972	3.00	28.0	*
1973-74	3.00	28.0	3.1
1975-76	1.50	15.0	3.1
1977-79	1.50	15.0	2.0
1980	0.41	7.0	2.0
1981	0.41	3.4	1.0

*No requirement

Source: Fearnsides et al. 1980, p. 18.

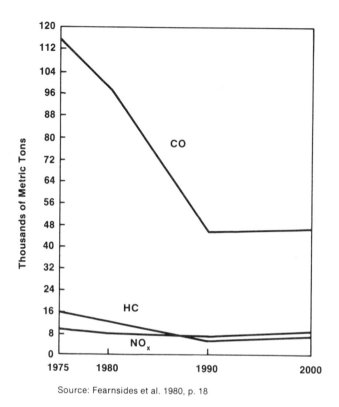

Source: Fearnsides et al. 1980, p. 18

This forecast was based on medium economic growth and status quo policies of NO_x control and a primarily gasoline-powered auto fleet was assumed. The forecasts were made by the National Transportation Policy Study Commission.

Figure 7.2
Daily Emissions from Urban Passenger Transportation

the Clean Air act provisions. The National Transportation Policy Study Commission forecasts a continuation of this trend through 1990 despite growth in the number of motor vehicles on the road. The projections in the figure are based on a scenario of moderate economic growth and a continuation of 1980 standards.

Although auto-emission regulations are an effective way of imposing air quality, they are not necessarily the best way to achieve the goal of improved air quality. Auto emissions are imposed by users of the automobile on the rest of the public. Thus, an ideal approach for achieving cleaner air would be to impose taxes or penalties on the user, depending on the automobile's level of pollution, its level of use, and its location. There have been numerous proposals of this type (Freeman, Haveman, and Kneese 1973; White 1976), but they have been ignored by Congress. In general the automobile emissions control policy has been one of "all cars must meet the same standard" at the factory gates or else stiff penalties will be imposed on the manufacturers. This approach ignores several factors such as regional considerations, emissions from older cars, and reduced travel and fuel use.

Regional Considerations

Population density, auto ownership, and environmental thresholds differ substantially across various locations in the United States. For instance, the need for auto-emissions control in Los Angeles is far more important than in Wichita, Kansas. Yet, Congress has forced the same standards on owners of automobiles in both of these areas.

Over 95 percent of vehicle trips made in the United States are under 16 miles in distance causing high levels of automobile pollution in densely populated areas. Thus, auto emissions relative to the assimilative capacity of the environment is a highly localized problem requiring solutions tailored to local conditions.

Emissions from Older Cars

The average age of cars has been steadily increasing in the past decade from 5.5 years in 1970 to 6.6 years in 1980. Thus, the concentration of older cars will be increasing progressively. Yet, there are very few laws, either local or national, to monitor the effectiveness of emission control devices over time. This ignores the fact that emissions are not only a function of the design of the automobile, but also of how well it is maintained.

Studies conducted for EPA on emissions from automobiles in actual use show that there is a significant deterioration in the control of emissions of hydrocarbons and carbon monoxide. Table 7.4 shows the percent by which a sample of automobiles in six cities exceeded the emission standards.

TABLE 7.4
Percent by which Sample Automobiles
Exceed Exhaust Emission Standards

Model Year	Number of Vehicles	Average Mileage	Percent Above Standard	
			HC	CO
1972	216	64,086	31	121
1973	240	55,245	30	120
1974	192	45,987	4	91
1975	262	38,010	53	120
1976	413	27,464	50	97
1977	636	16,478	7	57
1978	48	7,386	24	98

Note: Samples were taken in 1978 from six cities: Chicago, Denver, Houston, Phoenix, St. Louis, and Washington, D.C., except for model year 1978 which was from Denver and St. Louis only. The sample automobiles met the standards for emissions of nitrogen oxides in all cases.

Source: Automotive Testing Laboratories, 1979.

Reduced Travel and Fuel Use

The price of gasoline has virtually tripled in the past four years, and as a consequence vehicle miles traveled have declined by 2.5 percent since 1978. Gasoline consumption has declined even further, by almost 10 percent in the same period. Auto emissions standards, which were promulgated in 1977, do not make allowances for reduced travel or lower fuel use.

These factors point to a need for careful reconsideration of future emissions regulations. Given the national goal of achieving an ambient air quality which is in the best interests of public health and prevention of environmental deterioration, the important question is what is the most efficient way to achieve this? The burden of prevention of pollution must be shared by the automobile manufacturers and the users. Much of the current debate on automobile emission standards concerns the numerical targets of hydrocarbons, carbon monoxide, nitrogen oxides, and particulate levels rather than the issue of a target ambient air quality. Emissions standards are simply a means to achieve the goal of improved air quality.

ENERGY CONSERVATION REGULATION

In response to the Arab oil embargo in 1973 and the resultant adverse impacts on the domestic economy, the U.S. Congress passed the Energy Policy and Conservation Act (EPCA) in 1975. This act authorized the continued regulation of the domestic-oil price, which was originally imposed by the Nixon administration in the summer of 1971. The EPCA also authorized NHTSA to set fuel-efficiency standards on new cars and thereby help conserve petroleum. NHTSA established what are known as the Corporate Average Fuel Economy Standards (CAFE), which require automakers to meet the fuel-efficiency standards according to the schedule shown in Table 7.5. The corporate average is based on new car sales.

This regulation runs counter to the economic theory that the best way to conserve a commodity is to increase its price. The most expedient policy would be an excise tax on gasoline so that the price paid by consumers would be consistent with national objectives of fuel conservation. In the case of petroleum, however, Congress not only decided to regulate the price of gasoline, but also to regulate the automobile industry in order to offset the effect of the price regulation. The consequence was that consumers, facing low-regulated gasoline prices, started to demand large cars without

TABLE 7.5
Corporate Average Fuel Efficiency (CAFE) Standards

Model Year	Fuel Efficiency (Miles per Gallon)
1978	18[a]
1979	19[a]
1980	20[a]
1981	22[b]
1982	24[b]
1983	26[b]
1984	27[b]
1985	27.5[a]

[a]Set by Energy Policy and Conservation Act (EPCA) 1975.
[b]Set by the Secretary of Transportation in 1977 in compliance with EPCA.

Source: Fearnsides et al. 1980, p. 21.

regard to fuel economy. The auto industry had to pay cash rebates in January 1976 to sell subcompacts and close down production in several plants producing small cars. In addition, there was a substantial backlog of orders on V-8 engines.

The demand for large cars continued until consumers faced higher gasoline prices resulting from the Iranian crisis in early 1979. At that time there was a dramatic shift in consumer preference in favor of small cars. This relationship between small car preference and high gasoline prices is shown clearly in Figure 2.5 in Chapter 2. Had Congress deregulated domestic oil prices in 1975 and perhaps increased taxes on gasoline, then the transition to small cars would have proceeded in a more gradual manner. The domestic auto industry would have been partially insulated from the recent dramatic change in consumer demand. A strong case has been made that the current state of the U.S. auto industry is, to a substantial extent, due to the Energy Policy and Conservation Act (Tucker 1980). The problem with EPCA is that it did little to force consumers to demand small cars but instead forced the automakers to produce them.

At the present time, the automobile industry has exceeded the mandated Corporate Average Fuel Efficiency (CAFE) standards as a result of consumer preferences toward fuel-efficient small cars and the intense competition from imports in the small car market. As long as the price of gasoline remains high, this trend is likely to persist. Thus, there is very little justification for continued fuel economy regulation. The deregulation of domestic oil prices, initiated by former President Carter and finalized by the Reagan Administration in January 1981, has negated the need for fuel-efficiency regulations beyond 1985.

WORK PLACE REGULATIONS

In addition to product regulation, the auto industry is also subjected to regulation of their manufacturing facilities. These regulations include restrictions on air emissions, discharges into waterways, waste disposal, and worker safety. These fall under provisions of the Clean Air Act of 1963, the Clean Water Act of 1977, the Resource Conservation and Recovery Act of 1976 and the Occupational Safety and Health Act of 1970. Chrysler, which manufactures 10 percent of the cars produced in this country, estimates that these regulations will cost Chrysler over $550 million by 1985 (Auto Hearings 1981, p. 72).

In addition to the direct cost, regulations often create a major element of uncertainty in modernizing production facilities. One example is standards for pretreatment of industrial wastewater prior to discharge into municipal sewers. The standards are set for different categories of pollutants with compliance required at different times. Auto assembly facilities are affected by at least seven different wastewater categories. This necessitates redundant and duplicative water treatment to comply with each categorical standard as promulgated. Another example is the "Prevention of Significant Deterioration" (PSD) requirement of the 1977 Amendments to the Clean Air Act. This act requires a case-by-case review of permit applications to determine if new facilities can be built or old plants expanded. Onsite air quality monitoring is required before a permit can be granted. This may take many months and cost as much as $300,000 (General Motors 1981b).

Unlike regulations directed at the automobile, work place regulations do not affect foreign manufacturers. Many countries, particularly developing countries, are willing to accept lower standards of environmental quality and worker safety in order to promote industrialization. Thus, these regulations put U.S.-produced cars at a disadvantage against foreign-made cars, both in the United States and in the world markets.

In order to protect against this unfair advantage to foreign manufacturers, a tariff system could be instituted to equalize the advantage. It could be based on a "fair" market value which would include the cost of regulations that domestic automakers must comply with. It could be set individually by country considering each countries environmental standards and treatment of workers. Such a scheme would be similar to the tariff protection against dumping of steel.

CONCLUSIONS

Although there is some justification for past regulation of the automobile industry in the areas of safety and emissions, there is very little reason for continued regulation. Careful analyses are needed to determine if we have reached diminishing returns from improved designs in terms of auto safety and emissions. Perhaps it would be more effective to require users to maintain and operate their automobiles properly. Economic conditions have changed dramatically during the last decade. This change necessitates that numerical targets for emissions control at the tailpipe be reviewed in light of lower vehicle miles driven and the declining use of gasoline. Finally, serious consideration needs to be given to the idea of decentralizing the implementation of safety and environmental standards.

Appendix A
The AUTO1 Model

THEORY, STRUCTURE, AND ASSUMPTIONS

AUTO1 is a computer simulation model which captures the dynamics of the U.S. passenger car market.* AUTO1 is designed specifically to analyze the impact of alternate policies on the stability of the short-term transition in the auto industry. Stability is measured by the year-to-year fluctuations in sales and employment. Although there are several models of consumer demand for new cars currently available, none of them capture the interactions between the supply and the demand sectors of the U.S. passenger car industry, which is necessary in analyzing the impact of policies on sales and employment.† Furthermore, the AUTO1 model is unique as it incorporates the interactions between (1) used and new cars, (2) new car sales and inventories, (3) new car sales and industry capacity utilization, (4) industry profits and investment decisions, and (5) consumer choice between domestic and imported new cars. Causal feedbacks, non-linearity, and time lags are all explicitly represented in the model.

AUTO1 is based on a new theory of demand which explains some of the phenomena observed in the automobile market better than the standard neoclassical theory of demand. In the following section we present the neoclassical theory and identify its deficiencies. We then present the new theory of demand. We follow the theory section with a detailed description of the AUTO1 model,

---

*Development of AUTO1 was funded by the MITRE Corporation of McLean, Virginia [See Kannan, Rebibo, and Ellis (1981) for additional information].

†The Sweeney model at Stanford University, the Wharton model, and the INTRANS model at Dartmouth are some of the models of the automobile demand. A critical review of some of the vehicle choice models can be found in Tardiff (1980).

its structure, and assumptions. In Appendix B the model listing, definitions of variables, and model execution procedure are shown.

PASSENGER CARS AND THE THEORY OF DEMAND

Because of the importance of the automobile industry to the U.S. economy, passenger car demand has received much attention among economists. (For a detailed review of literature see Greene 1981.) Pioneering work by Chow (1957) and Nerlove (1957) in the 1950s developed what is known as the stock-adjustment approach to demand forecasting. This method focuses on the goal-seeking behavior of aggregate demand; that is, on the adjustment of actual automobile stocks to reach a certain long-term equilibrium of "desired stock." When a gap exists between the desired and actual stocks, an adjustment takes place in the form of new car purchases and/or retirements. The gap occurs because the total demand for cars increases, and old cars are discarded.

Until the energy crisis of 1973-74, the stock-adjustment approach dominated the field of automobile demand forecasting. This approach successfully explained the slow turnover rates in aggregate stocks in a manner similar to the way the demographic models explain population dynamics. This method, however, lacks a theoretically acceptable definition for automobile stocks. For instance, the concept of desired stocks lumps all types of vehicles from Lincolns to Chevrolets, regardless of their age, into a single demand category. Theoreticians could find no defensible way to justify aggregating all automobiles into a single demand category. Yet the practice persisted mainly because it could explain the behavior of automobile stocks successfully.

The Neoclassical Theory

After the energy crisis, interest in automobile demand forecasting was rekindled. Several attempts have been made to develop a theoretically sound method of forecasting automobile demand based on the neoclassical theory of consumer demand (Wykoff 1973; Hess 1977). According to this theory, the automobile is a durable good which provides a stream of services over its lifetime. The rational, utility-maximizing consumer treats the automobile as any other asset which he purchases to provide a service. Based on the consumer's budget and the relative prices of automobiles and other modes of transportation, the consumer will select an optimal combination of transportation services that maximizes his utility. The consumer utility is generally defined as a function of quantity of goods and services. Another way to look at it is to view the automobile as one of the assets in a consumer's portfolio which provides a flow of services over its lifetime. (For a detailed exposition of the neoclassical theory see Henderson and Quandt 1971, pp. 9-23.)

Although neoclassical models offers a more rigorous theoretical basis than stock-adjustment models, they fail to explain several important features of auto ownership. Unlike stock-adjustment models, neoclassical models do not adequately explain the slow turnover rates in the aggregate stock of automobiles. This is perhaps because the theory is principally applicable to modeling the decisions of individuals rather than the entire market as an aggregate unit (Greene 1981, pp. 1-75 and 1-76).

Furthermore, the neoclassical approach does not explain the large amount of idle capacity of personal automobiles and the lack of a rental market for this idle capacity. For instance, over half of all U.S. households own two or more cars, even though there is much idle capacity. This phenomenon of idle capacity seems to be true for most durable consumer goods (Harberger 1960). Analysts try to explain this deficiency in neoclassical theory by suggesting that the rental markets for automobiles are "underdeveloped" and thus consumers do not really have that choice (Smith 1975, p. 74; Wykoff 1973, pp. 377-378). Finally, the neoclassical theory does not explain the general reluctance among consumers to substitute mass transit for personal cars even when it is economically rational.

In our work we use a new theory called the "Access Theory of Demand." It explains the inertia in the stock turnover rates, the lack of rental markets for idle service capacity of cars, and the low propensity for successful substitution of mass transit for personal automobiles. Moreover, it offers a justification for the use of the stock-adjustment approach, which despite its success in helping explain these phenomena had hitherto lacked a rigorous theoretical basis.

The Access Theory of Demand*

The access theory of demand differs from the neoclassical theory in a fundamental way. The neoclassical theory assumes that rational consumers attempt to maximize their utility function subject to budget constraints. It is assumed that consumer preferences among the available choices are well known and invariant over time. For example, the choices of transportation services available to a consumer might be to purchase a new car with or without trading in an old car, to purchase a used car, to rent a car, or to use public transportation. The consumer is constantly faced with these choices and must choose the optimal mode of transportation along with all other goods and services.

In contrast, the access theory of demand assumes that consumers are uncertain about their preferences over time. In effect the ordering of individual consumer preferences may fluctuate from time to time. Thus, rational consumers, rather than choose one alternative over another, would attempt to maximize their "access" to a set of goods and services, subject, of course, to their budget constraints. For example, since consumers do not necessarily know in advance when they may desire to be mobile, they wish to have speedy access to transportation services. One way to ensure quick access is to own an automobile. If there were no budget constraints it would be reasonable to expect every licensed driver to own a personal automobile regardless of how many miles will be traveled. Thus, the new theory of demand emphasizes the attempt on the part of consumers to maximize their utility, which is defined as a function of access to the consumption of goods and services rather than the quantity consumed, as in the neoclassical theory.

If we assume that a consumer's desires change randomly over time, then the best way to maximize access to consumption of goods and services is by owning durable goods and holding inventories of nondurables. Thus, if budget constraints permit, there will be a discrepancy between the quantity demanded at the market price and the quantity actually consumed. This discrepancy shows up as inventories or as idle capacity depending on whether the

---

*The access theory of demand was developed by N. P. Kannan of Kannan and Associates, who also developed the AUTO1 model. For a more formal development of the theory, see Kannan (1981).

consumption item is nondurable or durable. In the case of the automobile, the consumer of transportation services may wish to purchase a car even if the vehicle will be idle over 90 percent of the time. On a rational basis, for instance, the consumer could save money by hiring a taxicab as needed but that would mean a sacrifice of instant access. Thus, the real tradeoff faced by consumers is between access to consumption of goods and services rather than between quantities. This perhaps explains why consumers usually choose to own rather than rent an automobile. Consequently, this is the cause for the lack of a rental market. From the viewpoint of the market for goods and services, the quantity demanded is what counts, not the quantity consumed. Although this distinction may vanish in the case of nondurables such as food and fuel, in the case of durable goods such as automobiles, it is significant.

The access theory of demand is more general and particularly more applicable to the case of consumer demand for automobiles than the neoclassical theory. The latter is too restrictive in its assumptions regarding the uncertainties a consumer faces over the relative value of alternate goods and services.

The access theory lends a theoretical basis to the stock-adjustment approach. The total stock of cars in use is determined by the demand for access to automobiles. Either new car purchases or retirements must adjust to make the total actual stocks and the desired stocks equal. Further, the problem of aggregating different types of automobiles into a single category of desired stock is diminished if each automobile is viewed primarily as an individual unit of transportation. The other attributes of the automobile that consumers may choose to purchase such as size, luxury, options, and style, are considered as separate goods and thus are not relevant to the definition of the desired stock.

THE AUTO1 MODEL STRUCTURE

In Figure A.1, a schematic diagram showing the basic sectors and their mutual interactions within the AUTO1 model is provided. On the demand side there are two equations that primarily govern the behavior of the model.

The first one determines the total demand for automobile stocks consistent with the access theory of demand, and the second

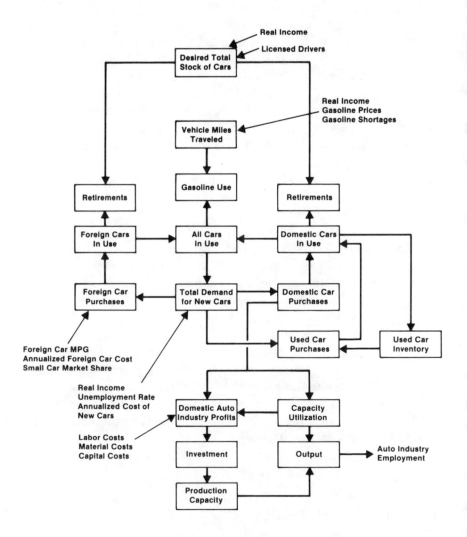

Figure A.1
A Schematic Representation of the AUTO1 Structure

126

determines the demand for new cars which is assumed to be independent of the total desired stocks. The scrappage rate is determined as the residual which equates the desired and the actual stocks. The basic demand equations are shown below.

$$\ln(d) = 3.969 + 0.472 \ln(l) + 0.67 \ln(i) \tag{1}$$
$$(1.38) \quad (0.12) \qquad (0.11)$$
Durbin Watson = 1.00 and R^2 = 0.995

$$\ln(s) = 15.21 + 1.92 \ln(i) - 1.99 \ln(c) - 0.002 \ln(u) \tag{2}$$
$$(1.25) \quad (0.2) \qquad (0.35) \qquad (0.0007)$$
Durbin Watson = 1.94 and R^2 = 0.927

where, d = the desired stock of automobiles
     l = number of licensed drivers
     i = real per capita disposable income in 1975 dollars
     s = sales of new cars
     c = weighted average annualized cost of new domestic
         and imported cars (1975 dollars/year)
     u = unemployment (percent change from previous year)

Ln is the natural logarithm, the terms under the coefficients are the standard errors of estimates, and R^2 is the coefficient of determination. The Durbin-Watson statistics provide a measure of serial correlation in independent variables. With exogenously specified values of real income, unemployment rate, and licensed drivers, these equations are used to specify the desired stock of automobiles and the demand for new cars.

The total new car sales is allocated between small and large cars exogenously. The small car market share is further allocated between domestic and foreign cars within the model using the fundamental equations of a Logit type model (see Rebibo et al. 1977, p. 10). The choice between domestic and foreign cars is assumed to be based on the relative annualized life cycle costs. The price, miles per gallon, and other attributes of foreign cars are specified exogenously whereas for domestic cars they are computed endogenously. Used car sales are determined as a function of new car sales and used car inventories, which in turn, is governed in the model by the rate of trade-ins. The rate of trade-ins is assumed to be proportional to new car sales. The used car sector in AUTO1 has been useful in testing policies which encourage trade-ins of old gas guzzlers. In the context of this work, we have not tested these policies as they are not directly relevant to the revitalization of the auto industry, but are primarily gasoline conservation measures.

The annualized cost of owning and operating an automobile is computed internally in the AUTO1 model using the price of new cars, interest rates, maintenance costs, gasoline prices, insurance, and taxes. Maintenance and gasoline costs are determined from the number of vehicle miles traveled, which is specified by the following equation that was estimated by Allen and Edmonds (1979, p. 14):

$$\ln(v) = 5.85 + 0.55 \ln(i) - 0.34 \ln(g) \tag{3}$$
$$\text{Durbin Watson} = 1.75 \text{ and } R^2 = 0.98$$

where v = vehicle miles traveled per licensed driver
        g = gasoline price index relative to the consumer price index
        i = real per capita disposable income in 1975 dollars

The supply side of the model consists of the adjustment of domestic auto industry production capacity to changes in new car sales and industry profits. Investment in new capacity is governed within the model by the demand for domestic cars and the rate of profit as a percent of revenues. The retail price of a new car is determined within the model on a cost plus margin basis which is adjusted with inventory levels. The factory cost of domestic cars is computed from several exogenous variables including the weight of the car, the average price per pound of materials, wages, man hours per car, the cost of special components, and the cost of environmental and safety regulations. These costs, along with the cost of capital when subtracted from the total revenues, determine the profits of the industry.

The model has a set of accounting relationships which keep track of stock of domestic cars, the average age, the average fuel efficiency, and the retirements.

AUTO1 BASE CASE

In Tables A.1 and A.2, the primary exogenous model assumptions are listed. The reader may wish to change any of these and

TABLE A.1
Major Base Case Assumptions

	History					Projections	
	1960	1965	1970	1975	1980	1985	1990
Small car market share (Percent)	25	22.5	34	45.5	64	77.5	80
Population (Million persons)	181	194	205	214	222	232	243
Licensed Drivers (Fraction of Population)	.483	.507	.544	.608	.655	.667	.680
Per Capita Real Disposable Income (1980 Dollars)	4,821	5,647	6,532	7,303	8,133	8,788	9,520
Gasoline Price Index (1972 = 100)	117.9	113.5	105.8	124.6	194.9	240.0	270.0
Unemployment* (Percent of U.S. Labor Force)	5.5	4.5	4.9	8.5	7.1	6.5	6.0
Imported Car Selling Price (1980 Dollars)	4,900	5,040	5,320	6,160	7,000	7,700	8,400
Imported New Car Average Miles Per Gallon	18	18	20	25	30	35	40

*Unemployment is assumed to reach a high of 9 percent in 1982 before decreasing. The model actually uses percent change from previous year.

Sources: Small car market share – National Automobile Dealer's Association, 1981. The projections were estimated by the authors. Population – Series II Projections, U.S. Bureau of the Census 1980. Licensed Drivers – Allen and Edmonds 1979. Disposable Income and Gasoline Price Index – Mid-Oil-price Scenario U.S. Department of Energy 1981, pp. 43 and 103. Unemployment – Historic values from Council of Economic Advisors 1981, p. 269, projected values assumed. Imported car price and MPG – assumed values.

TABLE A.2
Auto Industry Related Assumptions

	History					Projections	
	1960	1965	1970	1975	1980	1985	1990
Capacity Replacement Costs (1980 Dollars/car/year)	5,600	5,600	5,600	5,600	5,600	5,600	5,600
Productivity (Manhours/Car)	235	192	179	143	140	130	120
Wage Rate (1980 Dollars/hour)	9.50	10.20	11.20	13.30	15.40	16.80	18.20
Inertial Weight (Pounds/car)	3,500	3,550	3,850	4,200	3,100	2,700	2,400
Material Costs (1980 Dollars/Pound)	0.38	0.36	0.36	0.36	0.39	0.42	0.45
Special Component Costs (1980 Dollars/Car)	84	280	560	910	1,120	1,190	1,190

Sources: Capacity — Federal Task Force 1976. Productivity — U.S. International Trade Commission 1980; U.S. Department of Labor 1978. Wage Rate — Estimated from U.S. Department of Labor 1979. Weight — Environmental Protection Agency 1980; Paine Webber 1980. Material Cost — Federal Task Force 1976. Special Component Cost (includes cost of environmental and safety regulations) — Federal Task Force 1976; U.S. Bureau of the Census 1980; Estimates on future regulatory costs.

test for implications using the AUTO1 model. In fact, this is precisely the purpose of the model. It simply provides a structure for testing implications on sales and employment in the U.S. auto industry of alternate exogenous assumptions.

The small car share of the domestic market is assumed to increase from the current level of 64 percent to 80 percent by 1990. The demand for new cars is derived from the real per capita disposable income, the number of licensed drivers, and the rate of unemployment. Disposable income is perhaps one of the most critical and uncertain variables in the model. In the base case disposable income is almost constant (in real terms) between 1979 and 1982 and then rises at a modest 2.0 percent per year to 1990. Unemployment in the base case is assumed to decline from the current rate of almost 9 percent per year to 6 percent per year. The number of licensed drivers is assumed to grow at a rate slightly greater than the population. Another important exogenous variable is the price of gasoline. This is used in computing the vehicle miles driven per licensed driver and the annualized cost of owning and operating an automobile. Assumptions on the future price of gasoline are taken from projections made by the Energy Information Administration and are consistent with the base case assumptions used here on disposable income and unemployment (U.S. Department of Energy 1980, pp. 43 and 103, mid-price scenario).

A plot of the historical behavior of a selected set of variables is shown in Figure A.2 along with model-generated values of the same variables. The close correspondence between actual and model-generated values provides us with one measure of establishing confidence in the behavior of the AUTO1 model. Since we are mostly interested in the cyclical behavior relating to stability of transition and fluctuations rather than the precise predictions of sales or employment, we did not subject the model predictions to a rigorous statistical test.

The base case projections, which, in our opinion, reflects the most likely evolution of the auto industry in the next five to seven years (Figure A.3). The base case includes current government policies such as import quota on Japanese autos and regulatory relief. In Chapter 4 of this volume we presented the projected fluctuations in auto industry employment in the base case. It incorporates all the assumptions listed earlier in Tables A.1 and A.2.

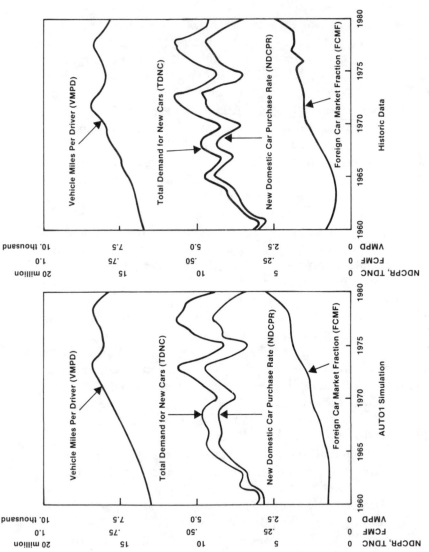

Source: AUTO1 Model Projections : Motor Vehicle Manufacturers Association 1981

Figure A.2
Comparison of AUTO1 Simulation with History

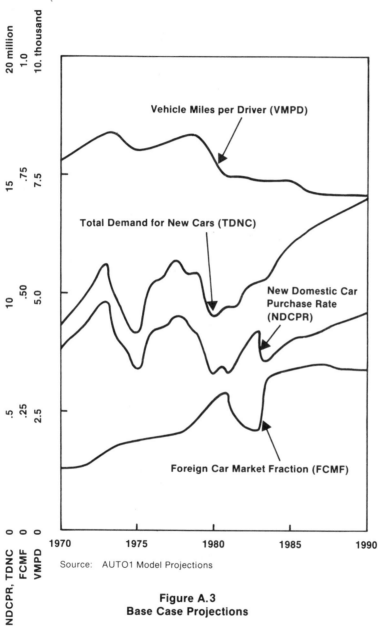

Source: AUTO1 Model Projections

Figure A.3
Base Case Projections

The following variables were chosen to illustrate the base case projection:

1. Total new car sales
2. Domestic new car sales
3. Imported car sales as a fraction of total U.S. car sales
4. Average miles traveled per driver

Several general observations can be made on the projected base case behavior. These are:

1. New passenger car sales in the U.S. (excluding light trucks) is projected to begin rising in 1982 and reach a level of 13 million units by 1990. The increase in new car sales follows from the assumption that real per capita disposable income will grow at an annual rate of two percent beginning in 1982.*

2. New domestic car sales are projected to rise in 1982 as a result of the rise in total sales and the import quota on Japanese cars. Sales drop off in 1983 when the quota is removed and then begin rising at the same rate as total car sales.

3. The foreign car share of the domestic market is likely to continue to rise to a long-term equilibrium level of 34 percent — up from the 1980 level of 26 percent. An exception to this is an expected two-year dip in 1982-83 due to the import quotas.

4. The average vehicle miles traveled per licensed driver is likely to decline to the mid-1960s level of 7100 miles per year. This is approximately 15 percent lower than the 1978 peak level and is mainly due to the assumptions of rising relative price of gasoline and a lower than historical rate of real income growth.

---

*This may be an optimistic estimate, given the current realities of stagnant real income growth, high unemployment, and high interest rates.

Appendix B

AUTO1 Model Listings, Variable Definitions, and Execution Procedure

THE DOCUMENTED LISTING OF THE AUTO1 MODEL

The AUTO1 model is written in Dynamo II and runs on the IBM/370 version of the compiler (Pugh 1977). Dynamo is a compiler for running continuous models described by a set of nonlinear differential equations.

In the listing, each group of equations is followed by a list of the variables appearing in the equations and their definitions. The letter to the right of the sequence number on each equation indicates the dynamo statement type These are:

A — auxiliary
C — constant
L — level
N — initial value
R — rate
T — table

```
************************************************************
VERSION RELEASE DATE APRIL 1982
************************************************************
***********SPECIFICATION OF EXOGENOUS INPUTS**************
************************************************************
POPULATION AND LICENSED DRIVERS
************************************************************
```

```
POP.K=CLIP(POP1.K,POP2.K,TIME.K,1980)                    11, A
POP1.K=TABHL(POP1T,TIME.K,1980,2000,5)*1E6               12, A
POP1T=222/232/243/252/260                                13, T
POP2.K=TABHL(POP2T,TIME.K,1960,1980,1)*1E6               14, A
POP2T=180.7/183.7/186.6/189.2/191.9/194.3/196.6/         15, T
   198.7/200.7/202.7/204.9/207.1/208.85/210.41/
   211.9/213.6/215.2/216.9/218.5/220.8/222
      POP    - US POPULATION (PERSONS)
      POP1   - US POPULATION - 1980-2000
      POP2   - US POPULATION - 1960-1980
      TIME   - SIMULATION TIME IN YEARS
      POP1T  - POP1 TABLE
      POP2T  - POP2 TABLE
```

```
LICENSED DRIVERS
```

```
LDFP.K=CLIP(LDFP1.K,LDFP2.K,TIME.K,1980)                 21, A
LDFP1.K=TABHL(LDFP1T,TIME.K,1980,2000,10)                22, A
LDFP1T=.655/.68/.71                                      23, T
LDFP2.K=TABHL(LDFP2T,TIME.K,1960,1980,1)                 24, A
LDFP2T=.483/.483/.485/.495/.497/.507/.514/.519/          25, T
   .525/.534/.544/.550/.565/.580/.589/.608/.620/
   .630/.635/.64/.655
LD.K=POP.K*LDFP.K                                         28, A
      LDFP   - LICENSED DRIVERS AS A FRACTION OF
                  POPULATION
      LDFP1  - LICENSED DRIVER FRACTION 1980-2000
      LDFP2  - LICENSED DRIVER FRACTION 1960-1980
      TIME   - SIMULATION TIME IN YEARS
      LDFP1T - LDFP1 TABLE
      LDFP2T - LDFP2 TABLE
      LD     - NUMBER OF LICENSED DRIVERS
      POP    - US POPULATION (PERSONS)
```

UNEMPLOYMENT RATE - PERCENT CHANGE FROM PREVIOUS YEAR

```
URPCPY.K=CLIP(URPCPY1.K,URPCPY2.K,TIME.K,1980)      32, A
URPCPY2.K=TABHL(URPCT2,TIME.K,1960,1980,1)          33, A
URPCT2=0/21.82/-17.91/3.64/-8.77/-13.46/-15.55/0/   34, T
  -5.263/-2.78/40.0/20.41/-5.08/-12.5/14.28/51.78/
  -9.41/-9.09/-14.28/-3.34/22.41
URPCPY1.K=TABHL(URPCT1,TIME.K,1980,1990,1)          37, A
URPCT1=22.41/6.25/3.5/-9/-6/-6/0/0/0/0/0            38, T
     URPCPY - UNEMPLOYMENT RATE PERCENT CHANGE FROM
                   PREVIOUS YR.(%)
     URPCPY1- UNEMPLOYMENT RATE PERCENT CHANGE FROM
                 PREV.YR, 1980-90
     URPCPY2- UNEMPLOYMENT RATE PERCENT CHANGE FROM
                 PREV.YR, 1960-80
     TIME    - SIMULATION TIME IN YEARS
     URPCT2  - URPCPY2 TABLE
     URPCT1  - URPCPY1 TABLE
```

REAL PERCAPITA DISPOSABLE INCOME(1975$)
        TABLE DATA IS IN 1972$

```
RPCDI.K=CLIP(RPCDI2.K,RPCDI1.K,TIME.K,1980)*RIPI75  43, A
RPCDI1.K=TABHL(RPCDI1T,TIME.K,1960,1980,1)*1E3      44, A
RPCDI1T=2.707/2.742/2.813/2.865/3.026/3.171/3.290/  45, T
  3.389/3.493/3.564/3.668/3.763/3.880/4.112/4.050/
  4.101/4.216/4.332/4.487/4.584/4.567
RPCDI2.K=TABHL(RPCDI2T,TIME.K,1980,2000,2)*1E3      48, A
RPCDI2T=4.567/4.570/4.77/5.1/5.20/5.346/5.680/      49, T
  5.890/6.10/6.47/6.76
RIPI75=1.272                                        51, C
     RPCDI  - REAL PER CAPITA DISPOSABLE INCOME
                 (1975$/YEAR)
     RPCDI2 - REAL PER CAPITA DISPOSABLE INCOME 1980-2000
     RPCDI1 - REAL PER-CAPITA DISPOSABLE INCOME 1960-1980
     TIME    - SIMULATION TIME IN YEARS
     RIPI75 - CONVERSION FACTOR FROM 1972 TO 1975 DOLLARS
     RPCDI1T- RPCDI1 TABLE
     RPCDI2T- RPCDI2 TABLE
```

GASOLINE AND OIL PRICE INDEX

```
GASPI.K=CLIP(GASPI2.K,GASPI1.K,TIME.K,1980)/GASPI75   55, A
GASPI75=1.246                                         56, C
GASPI1.K=TABHL(GASPI1T,TIME.K,1960,1980,1)            57, A
GASPI1T=117.9/115.7/114.8/113.1/111.5/113.5/112.9/    58, T
   113.7/110.9/109.6/105.8/102.2/100/103.4/126.4/
   124.6/123.4/123.7/120.0/147.6/194.9
GASPI2.K=TABHL(GASPI2T,TIME.K,1980,2000,2)            61, A
GASPI2T=194.9/190/200/260/265/270/270/270/270/270/    62, T
   270
      GASPI  - GASOLINE PRICE INDEX (1975=100)
      GASPI2 - GASOLINE PRICE INDEX 1980-2000
      GASPI1 - GASOLINE PRICE INDEX 1960-1980
      TIME   - SIMULATION TIME IN YEARS
      GASPI75- CONVERSION FACTOR TO 1975 BASE YEAR
      GASPI1T- GASPI1 TABLE
      GASPI2T- GASPI2 TABLE
```

GASOLINE PRICE PER GALLON, GAS TAXES, AND SHORTAGES

```
GASP.K=((GASP75*GASPI.K)/100)+(GASTAX.K)              67, A
GASP75=0.50                                           68, C
GSTXREV.K=GASTAX.K*TGASCO.K                           69, A
GASTAX.K=TABHL(GASTAB,TIME.K,1981,2000,1)             70, A
GASTAB=0/0/0/0/0/0/0/0/0/0/0/0/0/0/0/0/0/0/0/0        71, T
      GASP    - GASOLINE PRICE (1975$/GALLON)
      GASP75  - GASOLINE PRICE IN 1975 (1975$/GALLON)
      GASPI   - GASOLINE PRICE INDEX (1975=100)
      GASTAX  - GASOLINE TAX (1975$/GALLON)
      GSTXREV - GAS-TAX REVENUES TO GOVERNMENT (1975$)
      TGASCO  - TOTAL GASOLINE CONSUMED (GALLONS/YEAR)
      GASTAB  - GASOLINE TAX TABLE
      TIME    - SIMULATION TIME IN YEARS
```

GAS PRICE INDEX WITH GAS TAX

```
GASPIX.K=(GASP.K/GASP75)*100                          75, A
      GASPIX - GASOLINE PRICE INDEX WITH TAX
      GASP   - GASOLINE PRICE (1975$/GALLON)
      GASP75 - GASOLINE PRICE IN 1975 (1975$/GALLON)
```

GASOLINE SHORTAGES

```
GSHORT.K=1-STEP(0.05,1973.9)+STEP(0.05,1974.2)-       79, A
   STEP(0.05,1979.1)+STEP(0.05,1979.3)-STEP(SF,SYR)+
   STEP(SF,SYR+SD)
SF=0.10                                               82, C
SYR=2100                                              83, C
SD=0.5                                                84, C
      GSHORT - FRACTION OF VMT DEMAND UNSATISFIED BY
                   GASOLINE SHORTAGE
      SF     - FRACTION OF GASOLINE DEMAND UNSATISFIED
                   FROM SHORTAGE
      SYR    - GASOLINE SHORTAGE YEAR
      SD     - DURATION OF GASOLINE SHORTAGE (YEARS)
```

SMALL CAR MARKET SHARE

```
SCMSF.K=TABHL(SCMSFT,TIME.K,1960,1990,2)              88, A
SCMSFT=0.25/0.23/0.2/0.25/0.28/0.34/0.355/0.44/      89, T
  0.47/0.48/0.64/0.7/0.75/0.8/0.8/0.8
     SCMSF  - SMALL CAR MARKET SHARE FRACTION OF TOTAL
              U.S. MARKET
     SCMSFT - SMALL CAR MARKET SHARE TABLE
     TIME   - SIMULATION TIME IN YEARS
```

VEHICLE MILES PER REGISTERED DRIVER -TRAVEL DEMAND

```
VMPRD.K=SMOOTH((A)*(EXP(ALP*LOGN(RPCDI.K)))*         94, A
  (EXP(BET*LOGN(GASPIX.K)))*(GSHORT.K),1)
VMPRD=6600                                           96, N
A=347                                                97, C
ALP=0.55                                             98, C
BET=-0.34                                            99, C
     VMPRD  - VEHICLE MILES PER REGISTERED DRIVER (MILES/
              DRIVER/YEAR)
     A      - CONSTANT TERM IN VMPRD EQUATION
     ALP    - INCOME ELASTICITY PARAMETER FOR VMPRD
     RPCDI  - REAL PER CAPITA DISPOSABLE INCOME
              (1975$/YEAR)
     BET    - PRICE ELASTICITY PARAMETER FOR VMPRD
     GASPIX - GASOLINE PRICE INDEX WITH TAX
     GSHORT - FRACTION OF VMT DEMAND UNSATISFIED BY
              GASOLINE SHORTAGE
```

TOTAL VMT DEMAND

```
TVMT.K=LD.K*VMPRD.K                                 103, A
     TVMT   - TOTAL VEHICLE MILES TRAVELLED BY CARS
              (MILES/YEAR)
     LD     - NUMBER OF LICENSED DRIVERS
     VMPRD  - VEHICLE MILES PER REGISTERED DRIVER (MILES/
              DRIVER/YEAR)
```

***********STOCKS OF CARS IN USE***********
FOREIGN CARS IN USE

```
FCIU.K=FCIU.J+(DT)(FCPR.JK-FCRR.JK)                 110, L
FCIU=1.5E6                                          111, N
FCRR.KL=(FCIU.K/TCIU.K)*TRET.K                      112, R
TRET.K=MAX(0,(TCIU.K+TDNC.K-DTSOC.K))               113, A
     FCIU   - FOREIGN CARS IN USE (CARS)
     FCPR   - FOREIGN CAR PURCHASE RATE (CARS/YEAR)
     FCRR   - FOREIGN CAR RETIREMENT RATE (CARS/YEAR)
     TCIU   - TOTAL CARS IN USE (CARS)
     TRET   - TOTAL RETIREMENTS (SCRAP) OF CARS (CARS/
              YEAR)
     TDNC   - TOTAL DEMAND FOR NEW CARS (CARS/YEAR)
     DTSOC  - DESIRED TOTAL STOCK OF CARS (CARS)
```

AVERAGE LIFE OF CAR

```
ALC.K=TABHL(ALCT,AMTPV.K/AMTPVN,0,2,.2)*ALCN          117, A
ALCT=1.5/1.4/1.3/1.2/1.1/1/.9/.8/.7/.6/.5             118, T
ALCN=12                                               119, C
AMTPVN=10000                                          120, C
AMTPV.K=TVMT.K/TCIU.K                                 121, A
TCIU.K=FCIU.K+DCIU.K                                  122, A
```
```
     ALC    - AVG LIFE OF CAR (YEARS)
     ALCT   - AVERAGE LIFE OF CAR TABLE
     AMTPV  - AVG MILES TRAVELLED PER VEHICLE (MILES/
                 YEAR)
     AMTPVN - AVG MILES TRAVELLED PER VEHICLE NORMAL
                 (MILES/YEAR)
     ALCN   - AVERAGE LIFE OF CAR NORMAL (YEARS)
     TVMT   - TOTAL VEHICLE MILES TRAVELLED BY CARS
                 (MILES/YEAR)
     TCIU   - TOTAL CARS IN USE (CARS)
     FCIU   - FOREIGN CARS IN USE (CARS)
     DCIU   - DOMESTIC CARS IN USE (CARS)
```

DOMESTIC CARS IN USE

```
DCIU.K=DCIU.J+(DT)(DNCSR.JK+UDCPR.JK-RAUDCI.JK-       126, L
   DCRR.JK)
DCIU=55.5E6                                           127, N
```
```
     DCIU   - DOMESTIC CARS IN USE (CARS)
     DNCSR  - DOMESTIC NEW CAR SALES RATE (CARS/YEAR)
     UDCPR  - USED DOMESTIC CAR PURCHASE RATE (CARS/YEAR)
     RAUDCI - RATE OF ADDITIONS TO USED DOMESTIC CAR
                 INVENTORIES (CARS/YR)
     DCRR   - DOMESTIC CAR RETIREMENT RATE (CARS/YEAR)
```

AVERAGE MPG OF CARS IN USE

```
AMPGAC.K=(AMPGFC.K*FCIU.K+AMPGDC.K*DCIU.K)/TCIU.K      131, A
AMPGFC.K=AMPGFC.J+(DT)(AMPGFCR.JK)                     132, L
AMPGFCR.KL=((AMPGFC.K*(FCIU.K*(1-(1/ALC.K)))+          133, R
  FCPR.JK*MPGNFC.K)/(FCIU.K*(1-(1/ALC.K))+FCPR.JK))
  -AMPGFC.K
AMPGFC=18                                              136, N
AMPGDC.K=AMPGDC.J+(DT)(AMPGDCR.JK)                     137, L
AMPGDCR.KL=((AMPGDC.K*(DCIU.K*(1-(1/ALC.K))-DCER.K)    138, R
  +UCNCUR*UDCPR.JK*AMPGUDC.K-RAUDCI.JK*AMPGDC.K+
  NDCPR.JK*MPGNDC.K)/(DCIU.K*(1-(1/ALC.K))-DCER.K+
  NDCPR.JK-RAUDCI.JK+UDCPR.JK))-AMPGDC.K
AMPGDC=14                                              142, N
AMPGUDC.K=AMPGUDC.J+(DT)(AMPGUCR.JK)                   143, L
AMPGUDC=15                                             144, N
AMPGUCR.KL=((AMPGUDC.K*(UDCI.K-UDCPR.JK)+RAUDCI.JK*    145, R
  SMOOTH(MPGNDC.K,ALC.K/2))/(UDCI.K-UDCPR.JK+
  RAUDCI.JK))-AMPGUDC.K
```

```
     AMPGAC  - AVERAGE MPG OF ALL CARS ON THE ROAD
     AMPGFC  - AVG MPG OF FOREIGN CARS IN USE
     FCIU    - FOREIGN CARS IN USE (CARS)
     AMPGDC  - AVG MPG OF DOMESTIC CARS IN USE
     DCIU    - DOMESTIC CARS IN USE (CARS)
     TCIU    - TOTAL CARS IN USE (CARS)
     AMPGFCR - AVG MPG OF FOREIGN CARS - CHANGE RATE
     ALC     - AVG LIFE OF CAR (YEARS)
     FCPR    - FOREIGN CAR PURCHASE RATE (CARS/YEAR)
     MPGNFC  - MPG OF NEW FOREIGN CARS
     AMPGDCR - AVG MPG OF DOMESTIC CARS - CHANGE RATE
     DCER    - DOMESTIC CAR EARLY RETIREMENTS (CARS/YEAR)
     UCNCUR  - USED CAR NORMAL USAGE RATE AS A FRACTION OF
               NEW CAR USE
     UDCPR   - USED DOMESTIC CAR PURCHASE RATE (CARS/YEAR)
     AMPGUDC - AVG MPG OF USED DOMESTIC CARS
     RAUDCI  - RATE OF ADDITIONS TO USED DOMESTIC CAR
               INVENTORIES (CARS/YR)
     NDCPR   - NEW DOMESTIC CAR PURCHASE RATE (UNIT
               ORDERS/YEAR)
     MPGNDC  - MPG OF NEW DOMESTIC CARS
     AMPGUCR - AVG MPG OF USED DOMESTIC CARS - CHANGE RATE
     UDCI    - USED DOMESTIC CAR INVENTORY (CARS)
```

TOTAL GASOLINE CONSUMPTION

```
TGASCO.K=GASCFC.K+GASCDC.K                              151, A
GASCFC.K=(FCIU.K*AMTPV.K)/AMPGFC.K                      152, A
GASCDC.K=(DCIU.K*AMTPV.K)/AMPGDC.K                      153, A
TQUAGC.K=TGASCO.K/GPQ                                   154, A
GPQ=6.8E9                                               155, C
TCQUAC.K=TCQUAC.J+(DT)(TCQUACR.JK)                      156, L
TCQUAC=0                                                157, N
TCQUACR.KL=STEP(1,1981)*TQUAGC.K                        158, R
    TGASCO - TOTAL GASOLINE CONSUMED (GALLONS/YEAR)
    GASCFC - GASOLINE CONSUMED BY FOREIGN CARS (GALLONS/
             YEAR)
    GASCDC - GASOLINE CONSUMED BY DOMESTIC CARS
             (GALLONS/YEAR)
    FCIU   - FOREIGN CARS IN USE (CARS)
    AMTPV  - AVG MILES TRAVELLED PER VEHICLE (MILES/
             YEAR)
    AMPGFC - AVG MPG OF FOREIGN CARS IN USE
    DCIU   - DOMESTIC CARS IN USE (CARS)
    AMPGDC - AVG MPG OF DOMESTIC CARS IN USE
    TQUAGC - TOTAL QUADS OF GASOLINE CONSUMED (QUADS/
             YEAR)
    GPQ    - GALLONS OF GASOLINE PER QUAD
    TCQUAC - TOTAL CUMULATIVE QUADS CONSUMED (QUADS)
    TCQUACR- TOTAL CUMULATIVE QUADS CONSUMED - CHANGE
             RATE
```

AVERAGE AGE OF CARS IN USE

```
AAAC.K=(AAFC.K*FCIU.K+AADC.K*DCIU.K)/TCIU.K          162, A
AAFC.K=AAFC.J+(DT)(AAFCCR.JK)                        163, L
AAFC=5                                              164, N
AAFCCR.KL=((FCIU.K*AAFC1.K*(1-(1/ALC.K)))/(FCIU.K*  165, R
 (1-(1/ALC.K))+FCPR.JK))-AAFC.K
AAFC1.K=AAFC.K+1                                     167, A
AADC.K=AADC.J+(DT)(AADCCR.JK)                        168, L
AADC=6                                              169, N
AADCCR.KL=((DCIU.K*AADC1.K*(1-(1/ALC.K))-RAUDCI.JK* 170, R
 AADC1.K+AAUCI.K*UDCPR.JK)/(DCIU.K*(1-(1/ALC.K))-
 DCER.K+NDCPR.JK+UDCPR.JK-RAUDCI.JK))-AADC.K
AADC1.K=AADC.K+1                                     174, A
AAUCI.K=AAUCI.J+(DT)(AAUCIR.JK)                      175, L
AAUCI=6                                             176, N
AAUCIR.KL=((AAUC1.K*UDCI.K-AAUC1.K*UDCPR.JK+AADC.K* 177, R
 RAUDCI.JK)/(UDCI.K-UDCPR.JK+RAUDCI.JK))-AAUCI.K
AAUC1.K=AAUCI.K+1                                    180, A
```

```
    AAAC    - AVERAGE AGE OF ALL CARS ON THE ROAD (YEARS)
    AAFC    - AVERAGE AGE OF FOREIGN CARS ON THE ROAD
                (YEARS)
    FCIU    - FOREIGN CARS IN USE (CARS)
    AADC    - AVERAGE AGE OF DOMESTIC CARS ON THE ROAD
                (YEARS)
    DCIU    - DOMESTIC CARS IN USE (CARS)
    TCIU    - TOTAL CARS IN USE (CARS)
    AAFCCR  - AVERAGE AGE OF FOREIGN CARS CHANGE RATE
    AAFC1   - AN INTERMEDIATE AUXILLARY VARIABLE
    ALC     - AVG LIFE OF CAR (YEARS)
    FCPR    - FOREIGN CAR PURCHASE RATE (CARS/YEAR)
    AADCCR  - AVERAGE AGE OF DOMESTIC CARS CHANGE RATE
    AADC1   - AN INTERMEDIATE AUXILLARY VARIABLE
    RAUDCI  - RATE OF ADDITIONS TO USED DOMESTIC CAR
                INVENTORIES (CARS/YR)
    AAUCI   - AVERAGE AGE OF USED CARS IN INVENTORY
                (YEARS)
    UDCPR   - USED DOMESTIC CAR PURCHASE RATE (CARS/YEAR)
    DCER    - DOMESTIC CAR EARLY RETIREMENTS (CARS/YEAR)
    NDCPR   - NEW DOMESTIC CAR PURCHASE RATE (UNIT
                ORDERS/YEAR)
    AAUCIR  - AVERAGE AGE OF USED CARS IN INVENTORY
                CHANGE RATE
    AAUC1   - AN INTERMEDIATE AUXILLARY VARIABLE
  . UDCI    - USED DOMESTIC CAR INVENTORY (CARS)
```

```
************NEW CAR DEMAND SECTOR***********
NEW FOREIGN CAR SALES

FCPR.KL=MIN(FCPR1.K,FCPR2.K)                        186, R
FCPR1.K=TDNC.K*FCMF.K                               187, A
FCPR2.K=(FCPR1.K)*(1-STEP(1,IAQY)+STEP(1,IAQY+      188, A
  IAQD))+(IAQU)*(STEP(1,IAQY)-STEP(1,IAQY+IAQD))
IAQY=2100                                           190, C
IAQD=5                                              191, C
IAQU=2E6                                            192, C
    FCPR   - FOREIGN CAR PURCHASE RATE (CARS/YEAR)
    FCPR1  - FOREIGN CAR PURCHASE RATE WITH QUOTAS
             (CARS/YEAR)
    FCPR2  - FOREIGN CAR PURCHASE RATE WITHOUT QUOTAS
             (CARS/YEAR)
    TDNC   - TOTAL DEMAND FOR NEW CARS (CARS/YEAR)
    FCMF   - FOREIGN CAR MARKET CAPTURE FRACTION - TOTAL
             U.S MARKET
    IAQY   - IMPORT QUOTA BEGINNING YEAR
    IAQD   - IMPORT QUOTA DURATION (YEARS)
    IAQU   - IMPORT QUOTA CARS (CARS/YEAR)
```

NEW DOMESTIC CAR SALES

```
NDCPR.KL=TDNC.K-MIN(FCPR1.K,FCPR2.K)                  196, R
NDCPR=6E6                                             197, N
DCRR.KL=(DCIU.K/TCIU.K)*TRET.K+DCER.K                 198, R
RAUDCI.KL=MIN(NDCPR.JK,NTRADIN.K)                     199, R
RAUDCI=8E6                                            200, N
NTRADIN.K=DCIU.K*NTRADINF.K                           201, A
NTRADINF.K=TABHL(TRADT,AADC.K,0,7,1)                  202, A
TRADT=.112/.205/.205/.166/.117/.116/.116/.116         203, T
DCER.K=STEP(1,ACDEPYR)*DCER1.K-STEP(1,ACDEPYR+ACDT)   204, A
   *DCER1.K
ACDEPYR=2100                                          205, C
ACDT=5                                                206, C
DCER1.K=FDCRE.K*DCIU.K                                207, A
FDCRE.K=TABHL(FDCRET,DOITC.K,0,1,.2)                  208, A
FDCRET=0/.08/0.15/0.40/.8/1                           209, T
DOITC.K=TABHL(DOITCT,TIME.K,1981,1986,1)              210, A
DOITCT=0.10/0.2/0.2/0.2/0.2/0.1                       211, T
DCETI.K=STEP(1,ACTIPYR)*DCER1.K-STEP(1,ACTIPYR+       212, A
   ACTID)*DCER1.K
ACTIPYR=2100                                          213, C
ACTID=5                                               214, C
```

```
    NDCPR  - NEW DOMESTIC CAR PURCHASE RATE (UNIT
                  ORDERS/YEAR)
    TDNC   - TOTAL DEMAND FOR NEW CARS (CARS/YEAR)
    FCPR1  - FOREIGN CAR PURCHASE RATE WITH QUOTAS
                  (CARS/YEAR)
    FCPR2  - FOREIGN CAR PURCHASE RATE WITHOUT QUOTAS
                  (CARS/YEAR)
    DCRR   - DOMESTIC CAR RETIREMENT RATE (CARS/YEAR)
    DCIU   - DOMESTIC CARS IN USE (CARS)
    TCIU   - TOTAL CARS IN USE (CARS)
    TRET   - TOTAL RETIREMENTS (SCRAP) OF CARS (CARS/
                  YEAR)
    DCER   - DOMESTIC CAR EARLY RETIREMENTS (CARS/YEAR)
    RAUDCI - RATE OF ADDITIONS TO USED DOMESTIC CAR
                  INVENTORIES (CARS/YR)
    NTRADIN- NORMAL TRADE-INS OF USED CARS FOR NEW
                  DOMESTIC CARS (CARS/YR)
           - NORMAL TRADE-INS AS A FRACTION OF DOMESTIC
      *           CARS IN USE
    TRADT  - TRADE-IN FRACTION TABLE
    AADC   - AVERAGE AGE OF DOMESTIC CARS ON THE ROAD
                  (YEARS)
    ACDEPYR- ACCELERATED DEPRECIATION POLICY YEAR
    DCER1  - DOMESTIC CAR EARLY RETIREMENTS-INTERMEDIATE
                  VARIABLE
    ACDT   - ACCELERATED DEPRECIATION POLICY DURATION
                  (YEARS)
    FDCRE  - FRACTION OF DOMESTIC CARS RETIRED EARLY
    FDCRET - FRACTION RETIRED EARLY AS FUNCTION OF TAX
                  REBATE TABLE
    DOITC  - TAX CREDIT FOR TRADEIN/RETIRE OLD CAR FOR
                  NEW DOM.CARS
    DOITCT - DOITC(TAX CREDIT)TABLE
    TIME   - SIMULATION TIME IN YEARS
```

    DCETI - DOMESTIC CAR EARLY TRADEINS (CARS/YEAR)
    ACTIPYR- ACCELERATED TRADEIN POLICY YEAR
    ACTID - ACCELERATED TRADEIN POLICY DURATION (YEARS)

  FOREIGN CAR MARKET SHARE FRACTION

```
FCMFSC.K=FCMFSC.J+(DT)(FCMFCR.JK)                    218, L
FCMFSC=FCMFIN                                        219, N
FCMFIN=0.3                                           220, C
FCMFCR.KL=(IFCMFSC.K-FCMFSC.K)/FCMPD.K               221, R
FCMPD.K=TABHL(FCMPDT,CMF.K,0,.5,.05)                 222, A
FCMPDT=30/25/20/15/10/7/5/3/2/1/1                    223, T
CMF.K=FCIU.K/TCIU.K                                  224, A
IFCMFSC.K=TABHL(IFCMFT,SFDACR.K,0,2,.2)              225, A
IFCMFT=0.8/0.8/0.7/0.6/0.5/0.4/0.28/0.2/0.1/0.05/    226, T
  0.05
SFDACR.K=SMOOTH(ACFC.K/ACDC.K,DAT)                   227, A
DAT=1                                                228, C
FCMF.K=FCMFSC.K*SCMSF.K                              229, A
AFCMF.K=FCPR2.K/TDNC.K                               230, A
SAFCMF.K=SMOOTH(AFCMF.K,DAT)                         231, A
```

    FCMFSC - FOREIGN CAR MARKET CAPTURE FRACTION - U.S.
               SMALL CAR MKT.
    FCMFCR - FOREIGN CAR MARKET CAPTURE FRACTION CHANGE
               RATE-SMALL CAR MKT
    FCMFIN - FOREIGN CAR MARKET CAPTURE FRACTION INITIAL
               IN 1960 -SM.CAR.MKT
    IFCMFSC- INDICATED FOREIGN CAR MARKET FRACTION-SMALL
               CAR MARKET
    FCMPD - FOREIGN CAR MARKET PENETRATION DELAY
               (YEARS)
    FCMPDT - FOREIGN CAR MARKET PENETRATION DELAY TABLE
    CMF   - CURRENT MARKET FRACTION OF FOREIGN CARS TO
               TOTAL CARS IN USE
    FCIU   - FOREIGN CARS IN USE (CARS)
    TCIU   - TOTAL CARS IN USE (CARS)
    IFCMFT - INDICATED FOREIGN CAR MKT. FRACTION TABLE
    SFDACR - SMOOTHED FOREIGN TO DOMESTIC CAR ANNUALIZED
               COST RATIO
    ACFC   - ANNUALIZED COST OF FOREIGN CARS (1975$/YR/
               CAR)
    ACDC   - ANNUALIZED COST OF DOMESTIC CARS (1975$/YR/
               CAR)
    DAT   - DEMAND ADJUSTMENT TIME (YEARS)
    FCMF   - FOREIGN CAR MARKET CAPTURE FRACTION - TOTAL
               U.S MARKET
    SCMSF - SMALL CAR MARKET SHARE FRACTION OF TOTAL
               U.S. MARKET
    AFCMF - ACTUAL FOREIGN CAR MARKET SHARE FRACTION
               (FRACTION)
    FCPR2 - FOREIGN CAR PURCHASE RATE WITHOUT QUOTAS
               (CARS/YEAR)
    TDNC   - TOTAL DEMAND FOR NEW CARS (CARS/YEAR)
    SAFCMF - SMOOTHED ACTUAL FOREIGN CAR MARKET SHARE
               FRACTION

DEMAND FOR TOTAL STOCKS AND FOR NEW CARS

```
DTSOC.K=CONST*(EXP(ELD*LOGN(LD.K)))*(EXP(IE*          235, A
  LOGN(RPCDI.K)))
CONST=45                                              236, C
ELD=0.472                                             237, C
IE=0.67258                                            238, C
ACNC.K=FCWF.K*ACFC.K+(1-FCWF.K)*ACDC.K                239, A
FCWF.K=CLIP(SAFCMF.K,FCMF.K,TIME.K,IAQY)              240, A
TDNC.K=CX1*EXP(CX2+CX4*LOGN(RPCDI.K)+CX5*             241, A
  LOGN(ACNC.K)+CX6*URPCPY.K)+DCETI.K
CX1=1                                                 243, C
CX2=15.213                                            244, C
CX4=1.921                                             245, C
CX5=-1.9917                                           246, C
CX6=-0.00242                                          247, C
TDNC=6.641E6                                          248, N
```

```
    DTSOC  - DESIRED TOTAL STOCK OF CARS (CARS)
    CONST  - A CONSTANT TERM IN DTSOC EQUATION
    ELD    - ELASTICITY WRT. LICENSED DRIVERS IN DTSOC
               EQUATION
    LD     - NUMBER OF LICENSED DRIVERS
    IE     - INCOME ELASTICITY OF CAR-STOCK DEMAND
    RPCDI  - REAL PER CAPITA DISPOSABLE INCOME
               (1975$/YEAR)
    ACNC   - AVERAGE ANNUALIZED COST OF NEW CARS
               (1975$/YR/CAR)
    FCWF   - FOREIGN CAR WEIGHTAGE FACTOR IN ACNC
               EQUATION (FRACTION)
    ACFC   - ANNUALIZED COST OF FOREIGN CARS (1975$/YR/
               CAR)
    ACDC   - ANNUALIZED COST OF DOMESTIC CARS (1975$/YR/
               CAR)
    SAFCMF - SMOOTHED ACTUAL FOREIGN CAR MARKET SHARE
               FRACTION
    FCMF   - FOREIGN CAR MARKET CAPTURE FRACTION - TOTAL
               U.S MARKET
    TIME   - SIMULATION TIME IN YEARS
    IAQY   - IMPORT QUOTA BEGINNING YEAR
    TDNC   - TOTAL DEMAND FOR NEW CARS (CARS/YEAR)
    CX1    - A CONSTANT TERM IN TDNC EQUATION
    CX2    - A SECOND CONSTANT TERM IN TDNC EQUATION
    CX4    - REAL INCOME ELASTICITY OF NEW CAR DEMAND IN
               TDNC EQUATION
    CX5    - AVERAGE ANNUALIZED NEW CAR COST ELASTICITY
               OF NEW CAR DEMAND IN TDNC EQUATION
    CX6    - NEW CAR DEMAND ELASTICITY WRT. %CHANGE IN
               UNEMPLOYMENT FROM FROM PREVIOUS PERIOD
    URPCPY - UNEMPLOYMENT RATE PERCENT CHANGE FROM
               PREVIOUS YR.(%)
    DCETI  - DOMESTIC CAR EARLY TRADEINS (CARS/YEAR)
```

USED CAR MARKET SHARE FRACTION

```
UCMF.K=TABHL(UCMFT,NCUCCR.K,0,5,.5)                    252, A
UCMFT=0/0/1/1.2/1.4/1.6/1.8/2/2/2/2                    253, T
NCUCCR.K=SMOOTH(ACNC.K/ACUDC.K,DAT)                    254, A
NCUCCR=2.0                                             255, N
     UCMF   - USED CAR MARKET FRACTION
     UCMFT  - USED CAR MARKET FRACTION TABLE
     NCUCCR - NEW CAR USED CAR COST RATIO
     ACNC   - AVERAGE ANNUALIZED COST OF NEW CARS
              (1975$/YR/CAR)
     ACUDC  - ANNUALIZED COST OF USED DOMESTIC CARS
              (1975$/YR/CAR)
     DAT    - DEMAND ADJUSTMENT TIME (YEARS)
```

ANNUALIZED COST OF DOMESTIC CARS

```
ACDC.K=PPDC.K*FCRDC.K+PPDC.K*DTIFDC.K+OAMCDC.K+          259, A
  OGCDC.K
ACDC=3300                                               260, N
FCRDC.K=(INTDC.K)/(1-EXP(-FP.K*LOGN(1+INTDC.K)))        261, A
INTDC.K=INTC+STEP(0.01,1970)+STEP(0.02,1975)+           262, A
  STEP(0.02,1978)+STEP(0.02,1980)+STEP(0.02,1981)-
  STEP(0.02,1982)-STEP(INTPX,INTPYR)
INTPX=0.02                                              264, C
INTPYR=2100                                             265, C
INTC=0.03                                               266, C
FP.K=FPC                                                267, A
FPC=10                                                  268, C
DTIFDC.K=DTIFDCC                                         269, A
DTIFDCC=0.21                                            270, C
OAMCDC.K=SAMTPV.K*OAMPMDC                               271, A
OAMPMDC=0.02                                            272, C
OGCDC.K=(SAMTPV.K*GASP.K)/(MPGNDC.K)                    273, A
SAMTPV.K=SMOOTH(AMTPV.K,AUSC)                           274, A
AUSC=1                                                  275, C
```

    ACDC   - ANNUALIZED COST OF DOMESTIC CARS (1975$/YR/
                CAR)
    PPDC   - PURCHASE PRICE OF DOMESTIC CARS IN RETAIL
                (1975$/CAR)
    FCRDC   - FIXED CHARGE RATE FOR NEW DOMESTIC CARS
                (FRACTION/YR)
    DTIFDC - DEPRECIATION, TAXES, INSURANCE AS FRACTION
                OF INITIAL COSTS OF DOMESTIC CAR
    OAMCDC - OPERATING AND MAINTENANCE COSTS FOR
                DOMESTIC CAR (1975$/YEAR)
    OGCDC   - OIL AND GAS COST FOR DOMESTIC CAR
                (1975$/YR/CAR)
    INTDC   - INTEREST RATE FOR FINANCING NEW DOMESTIC
                CARS (FRACTION/YR)
    FP   - FINANCING PERIOD FOR NEW CARS (YEARS)
    INTC   - INTEREST RATE INITIAL (FRACTION/YR)
    INTPX   - INTEREST RATE SUBSIDY POLICY RATE
    INTPYR - INTEREST RATE SUBSIDY POLICY INITIATION
                YEAR
    FPC   - FINANCING PERIOD CONSTANT (YEARS)
    DTIFDCC- DTIFDC CONSTANT
    SAMTPV - SMOOTHED AVERAGE MILES TRAVELED PER VEHICLE
                (MILES/YEAR)
    OAMPMDC- OPERATING AND MAINTENANCE COST PER MILE -
                DOMESTIC CAR (75$/MI)
    GASP   - GASOLINE PRICE (1975$/GALLON)
    MPGNDC - MPG OF NEW DOMESTIC CARS
    AMTPV   - AVG MILES TRAVELLED PER VEHICLE (MILES/
                YEAR)
    AUSC   - AUTO USE SMOOTHING CONSTANT (YEARS)

149

ANNUALIZED COST OF FOREIGN CARS

```
ACFC.K=PPFC.K*FCRFC.K+PPFC.K*DTIFFC.K+OAMCFC.K+          279, A
   OGCFC.K
FCRFC.K=(INTFC.K)/(1-EXP(-FP.K*LOGN(1+INTFC.K)))        280, A
INTFC.K=INTDC.K+0.02                                    281, A
DTIFFC.K=DTIFFCC                                        282, A
DTIFFCC=0.2                                             283, C
OAMCFC.K=SAMTPV.K*OAMPMFC                               284, A
OAMPMFC=0.02                                            285, C
OGCFC.K=(SAMTPV.K*GASP.K)/(MPGNFC.K)                    286, A
```
      ACFC   - ANNUALIZED COST OF FOREIGN CARS (1975$/YR/
                  CAR)
      PPFC   - PURCHASE PRICE OF FOREIGN CARS IN RETAIL
                  (1975$/CAR)
      FCRFC - FIXED CHARGE RATE FOR FOREIGN CARS
                  (FRACTION/YR)
      DTIFFC - DEPRECIATION, TAXES, INSURANCE AS FRACTION
                  OF INITIAL COSTS OF FOREIGN CAR
      OAMCFC - OPERATING AND MAINTENANCE COSTS FOR FOREIGN
                  CAR (1975$/YEAR)
      OGCFC - OIL AND GAS COST FOR FOREIGN CAR
                  (1975$/YEAR/CAR)
      INTFC - INTEREST RATE FOR FINANCING FOREIGN CARS
                  (FRACTION/YEAR)
      FP   - FINANCING PERIOD FOR NEW CARS (YEARS)
      INTDC - INTEREST RATE FOR FINANCING NEW DOMESTIC
                  CARS (FRACTION/YR)
      DTIFFCC- DTIFFC CONSTANT
      SAMTPV - SMOOTHED AVERAGE MILES TRAVELED PER VEHICLE
                  (MILES/YEAR)
      OAMPMFC- OPERATING AND MAINTENANCE COST PER MILE -
                  FOREIGN CAR (75$/MI)
      GASP   - GASOLINE PRICE (1975$/GALLON)
      MPGNFC - MPG OF NEW FOREIGN CARS

   ***********USED CAR SECTOR***********
*
USED DOMESTIC CAR INVENTORY

```
UDCI.K=UDCI.J+(DT)(RAUDCI.JK-UDCPR.JK)                  293, L
UDCI=8E6                                                294, N
UDCPR.KL=MAX(0,UDCPX.K)                                 295, R
UDCPX.K=MIN(UDCI.K,DFUDC.K)                             296, A
DFUDC.K=TDNC.K*UCMF.K                                   297, A
UDCPR=8E6                                               298, N
```
      UDCI   - USED DOMESTIC CAR INVENTORY (CARS)
      RAUDCI - RATE OF ADDITIONS TO USED DOMESTIC CAR
                  INVENTORIES (CARS/YR)
      UDCPR - USED DOMESTIC CAR PURCHASE RATE (CARS/YEAR)
      UDCPX - USED DOMESTIC CAR INTERMEDIATE AUXILLIARY
                  VARIABLE (CARS/YR)
      DFUDC - DEMAND FOR USED DOMESTIC CARS (CARS/YEAR)
      TDNC   - TOTAL DEMAND FOR NEW CARS (CARS/YEAR)
      UCMF   - USED CAR MARKET FRACTION

AVERAGE PRICE OF USED DOMESTIC CARS

```
APUDC.K=DLINF3(PPDC.K,(ALC.K/2))*(EXP(-.23*AADC.K)) 302, A
   *MUDCICR.K
APUDC=1250                                            304, N
     APUDC  - AVG PRICE OF USED DOMESTIC CAR (1975$/CAR)
     PPDC   - PURCHASE PRICE OF DOMESTIC CARS IN RETAIL
              (1975$/CAR)
     ALC    - AVG LIFE OF CAR (YEARS)
     AADC   - AVERAGE AGE OF DOMESTIC CARS ON THE ROAD
              (YEARS)
     MUDCICR- MULTIPLIER FOR USED DOMESTIC CAR INVENTORY
              COVERAGE
```

USED CAR PRICE MULTIPLIER FROM INV. COVERAGE

```
MUDCICR.K=TABHL(MUDCT,(UDCI.K/(DFUDC.K+1))/        308, A
   UCINCN,0,2,.2)
MUDCT=5/3/2/1.4/1.1/1/0.9/0.8/0.7/0.6/0.5          309, T
UCINCN=0.1                                          310, C
     MUDCICR- MULTIPLIER FOR USED DOMESTIC CAR INVENTORY
              COVERAGE
     MUDCT  - MULTIPLIER FOR USED DOMESTIC CAR INVENTORY
              COVERAGE TABLE
     UDCI   - USED DOMESTIC CAR INVENTORY (CARS)
     DFUDC  - DEMAND FOR USED DOMESTIC CARS (CARS/YEAR)
     UCINCN - USED CAR INVENTORY COVERAGE NORMAL (YEARS)
```

ANNUALIZED COST OF USED DOMESTIC CARS

```
ACUDC.K=APUDC.K*FCRUC.K+APUDC.K*DTIFUDC.K+OAMCUC.K+    314, A
   OGCDCUC.K
FCRUC.K=(INTU.K)/(1-EXP(-FPUC.K*LOGN(1+INTU.K)))       316, A
INTU.K=INTDC.K+0.06                                    317, A
FPUC.K=ALC.K-AAUCI.K                                   318, A
DTIFUDC.K=DTIFUCC                                       319, A
DTIFUCC=0.15                                            320, C
OAMCUC.K=UCNCUR*SAMTPV.K*OAMCUCN                        321, A
UCNCUR=0.8                                              322, C
OAMCUCN=0.04                                            323, C
OGCDCUC.K=(UCNCUR*SAMTPV.K*GASP.K)/AMPGUDC.K            324, A
```

    ACUDC   - ANNUALIZED COST OF USED DOMESTIC CARS
                 (1975$/YR/CAR)
    APUDC   - AVG PRICE OF USED DOMESTIC CAR (1975$/CAR)
    FCRUC   - FIXED CHARGE RATE FOR USED CARS (FRACTION/
                 YEAR)
    DTIFUDC- DEPRECIATION, TAXES, INSURANCE AS FRACTION
                 OF INITIAL COST OF USED DOMESTIC CAR
    OAMCUC - OPERATING AND MAINTENANCE COST OF USED CAR
                 (1975$/YEAR)
    OGCDCUC- OIL AND GAS COST FOR DOMESTIC USED CAR
                 (1975$/YEAR/CAR)
    INTU   - INTEREST RATE FOR FINANCING USED CARS
                 (FRACTION/YR)
    FPUC   - FINANCING PERIOD FOR USED CARS (YEARS)
    INTDC   - INTEREST RATE FOR FINANCING NEW DOMESTIC
                 CARS (FRACTION/YR)
    ALC   - AVG LIFE OF CAR (YEARS)
    AAUCI   - AVERAGE AGE OF USED CARS IN INVENTORY
                 (YEARS)
    DTIFUCC- DTIFUDC CONSTANT
    UCNCUR - USED CAR NORMAL USAGE RATE AS A FRACTION OF
                 NEW CAR USE
    SAMTPV - SMOOTHED AVERAGE MILES TRAVELED PER VEHICLE
                 (MILES/YEAR)
    OAMCUCN- OPERATING AND MAINTENANCE COST FOR USED CAR
                 NORMAL (1975$/MI)
    GASP   - GASOLINE PRICE (1975$/GALLON)
    AMPGUDC- AVG MPG OF USED DOMESTIC CARS

```
***********DOMESTIC AUTO INDUSTRY SECTOR***********
DOMESTIC AUTO PRODUCTION SECTOR

DAPC.K=DAPC.J+(DT)(DAPCAR.JK-DAPCDR.JK-DAPCDIR.JK)    331, L
DAPC=6.5E6                                           332, N
DAPCDR.KL=DAPC.K/ALDAPC                              333, R
ALDAPC=20                                            334, C
DAPCDIR.KL=FRACD.K*DAPC.K                            335, R
FRACD.K=TABHL(FRACDT,SDAPCUF.K/NCUF,0,1,0.2)         336, A
FRACDT=0.6/0.6/0.3/0.2/0.1/0                         337, T
SDAPCUF.K=SMOOTH(DAPCUF.K,DCDISC)                    338, A
DCDISC=2                                             339, C
DAPCAR.KL=DELAY3(DAIC.K,DAFCT)                       340, R
DAFCT=1                                              341, C
DAIC.K=(DAIIF.K*DAREV.K*DAIMCU.K)/DACCR.K            342, A
DACCR.K=TABHL(DACCRT,TIME.K,1960,2000,5)*1E3         343, A
DACCRT=4/4/4/4/4/4/4/4/4                             344, T
DAIMCU.K=SMOOTH(DAPCUF.K/NCUF,CAPISC)                345, A
CAPISC=1                                             346, C
DAIIF.K=TABHL(DAIIFT,SRROS.K,0,2,.5)*DAIIFN          347, A
DAIIFT=0/0.5/.93/1.3/1.4                             348, T
DAIIFN=0.0537                                        349, C
SRROS.K=SMOOTH(DAROS.K/ARROS,ROSSC)                  350, A
ROSSC=2                                              351, C
ARROS=0.08                                           352, C
```

DAPC   - DOMESTIC AUTO INDUSTRY PRODUCTION CAPACITY
           (CARS/YEAR)
DAPCAR   - DOMESTIC AUTO PRODUCTION CAPACITY ADDITION
           RATE (CARS/YR/YR)
DAPCDR   - DOMESTIC AUTO PRODUCTION CAPACITY
           DEPRECIATION RATE (CARS/Y/Y)
DAPCDIR- DOMESTIC AUTO PROD. CAP. DISCARD RATE
           (CARS/YR/YR)
ALDAPC   - AVG LIFETIME OF DOMESTIC AUTO PRODUCTION
           CAPACITY (YEARS)
FRACD   - FRACTION OF CAPACITY DISCARDED (FRACTION/
           YR)
FRACDT   - FRACTION OF CAPACITY DISCARDED TABLE
SDAPCUF- SMOOTHED DOMESTIC AUTO PROD. CAPACITY UTIL.
           FACTOR
NCUF   - NORMAL CAPACITY UTILIZATION FACTOR
DAPCUF   - DOMESTIC AUTO PRODUCTION CAPACITY
           UTILIZATION FACTOR
DCDISC   - DOMESTIC CAPACITY DISCARD SMOOTHING
           CONSTANT (YEARS)
DAIC   - DOMESTIC AUTO INDUSTRY INVESTMENT IN
           CAPACITY (CARS/YR/YR)
DAFCT   - DOMESTIC AUTO AVG FACILITY CONSTRUCTION
           TIME (YEARS)
DAIIF   - DOMESTIC AUTO INDUSTRY INVESTMENT FRACTION
           (FRACTION/YR)
DAREV   - DOMESTIC AUTO REVENUES (1975$/YEAR)
DAIMCU   - DOMESTIC AUTO INVEST. MULTIPLIER FROM
           CAPACITY UTILIZATION
DACCR   - DOMESTIC AUTO CAPACITY COST RATIO
           (1975$/CAR/YEAR)
DACCRT   - DOMESTIC AUTO CAPACITY COST RATIO TABLE

```
    TIME    - SIMULATION TIME IN YEARS
    CAPISC  - CAPACITY UTILIZATION INVEST.MULTIPLIER
                SMOOTHING CONST (YRS)
    DAIIFT  - DOMESTIC AUTO INDUSTRY INVESTMENT FRACTION
                TABLE
    SRROS   - SMOOTHED RATE OF RETURN ON SALES (FRACTION/
                YEAR)
    DAIIFN  - DOMESTIC AUTO INDUSTRY INVESTMENT FRACTION
                NORMAL (FRAC./YR)
    DAROS   - DOMESTIC AUTO INDUSTRY RETURN ON SALES
                (FRACTION)
    ARROS   - AVG RATE OF RETURN ON SALES (FRACTION/YEAR)
    ROSSC   - RETURN ON SALES SMOOTHING CONSTANT (YEARS)
```

DOMESTIC AUTO IND. ACCOUNTING SECTOR

```
DAREV.K=NDCPR.JK*FPDC.K+GOVTINC.K                         356, A
GOVTINC.K=MAX(0,MPGNDC.K-RNCMPG.K)*250E6*GOVPYR.K         357, A
GOVPYR.K=STEP(1,GOVYR)-STEP(1,GOVYR+GOVPD)               358, A
GOVYR=2100                                               359, C
GOVPD=3                                                  360, C
DAROS.K=DAPRO.K/(DAREV.K+1)                              361, A
DAPRO.K=DAREV.K-DAICST.K                                 362, A
    DAREV   - DOMESTIC AUTO REVENUES (1975$/YEAR)
    NDCPR   - NEW DOMESTIC CAR PURCHASE RATE (UNIT
                ORDERS/YEAR)
    FPDC    - FACTORY PRICE OF DOMESTIC CARS (1975$/CAR)
    GOVTINC - GOVERNMENT INCENTIVES (1975$/YEAR)
    MPGNDC  - MPG OF NEW DOMESTIC CARS
    RNCMPG  - REGULATED NEW CAR MPG
    GOVPYR  - GOVERNMENT INCENTIVE POLICY YEARS
    GOVYR   - GOVERNMENT INCENTIVE POLICY BEGINNING YEAR
    GOVPD   - GOVERNMENT INCENTIVE POLICY DURATION
                (YEARS)
    DAROS   - DOMESTIC AUTO INDUSTRY RETURN ON SALES
                (FRACTION)
    DAPRO   - DOMESTIC AUTO INDUSTRY PROFITS (1975$/YEAR)
    DAICST  - DOMESTIC AUTO INDUSTRY COSTS (1975$/YR)
```

DOMESTIC AUTO INDUSTRY COSTS

```
DAICST.K=DAILC.K+DAIMC.K+SPCOMC.K+DAPC.K*FRACD.K*     366, A
   DACCR.K
DAICC.K=DAAST.K*DAIFCR                                367, A
DAAST.K=DAPC.K*DACCR.K                                368, A
DAIFCR=0.12                                           369, C
DAILC.K=DAILE.K*DAIWR.K                               370, A
DAILE.K=DAO.K*AMHPA.K                                 371, A
AMHPA.K=TABHL(AMHPAT,TIME.K,1960,2000,5)              372, A
AMHPAT=235/192/179/143/140/130/120/110/100           373, T
DAIWR.K=TABHL(DAIWRT,TIME.K,1960,2000,5)              374, A
DAIWRT=6.8/7.3/8.0/9.5/11/12/13/14/15                 375, T
DAIMC.K=DAO.K*LBSPC.K*COSTPLB.K                       376, A
LBSPC.K=TABHL(LBST,TIME.K,1960,2000,5)*1E3            377, A
LBST=3.5/3.55/3.85/4.2/3.1/2.7/2.4/2.1/2.0            378, T
COSTPLB.K=TABHL(COSTLBT,TIME.K,1960,2000,5)           379, A
COSTLBT=.27/.26/.26/.26/.28/.30/.32/.34/.35           380, T
SPCOMC.K=SPCOCPC.K*DAO.K                              381, A
SPCOCPC.K=TABHL(SPCOCPT,TIME.K,1960,2000,5)           382, A
SPCOCPT=60/200/400/650/800/850/850/850/850            383, T
```

```
     DAICST  - DOMESTIC AUTO INDUSTRY COSTS (1975$/YR)
     DAILC   - DOMESTIC AUTO INDUSTRY LABOR COSTS
               (1975$/YEAR)
     DAIMC   - DOMESTIC AUTO INDUSTRY MATERIAL COSTS
               (1975$/YEAR)
     SPCOMC  - SPECIAL COMPONENT COST FOR INDUSTRY
               (1975$/YEAR)
     DAPC    - DOMESTIC AUTO INDUSTRY PRODUCTION CAPACITY
               (CARS/YEAR)
     FRACD   - FRACTION OF CAPACITY DISCARDED (FRACTION/
               YR)
     DACCR   - DOMESTIC AUTO CAPACITY COST RATIO
               (1975$/CAR/YEAR)
     DAICC   - DOMESTIC AUTO INDUSTRY CAPITAL COSTS
               (1975$/YR)
     DAAST   - DOMESTIC AUTO INDUSTRY ASSETS (1975$)
     DAIFCR  - DOMESTIC AUTO INDUSTRY FIXED CHARGE RATE
               (FRACTION/YEAR)
     DAILE   - DOMESTIC AUTO INDUSTRY LABOR EMPLOYED (MAN-
               HOURS/YR)
     DAIWR   - DOMESTIC AUTO INDUSTRY WAGE RATE (1975$/MAN
               HOUR)
     DAO     - DOMESTIC AUTO OUTPUT (CARS/YEAR)
     AMHPA   - AVERAGE MAN-HOURS PER AUTO PRODUCTION (MAN-
               HOURS/CAR)
     AMHPAT  - AVG. MAN HOURS PER AUTO TABLE
     TIME    - SIMULATION TIME IN YEARS
     DAIWRT  - DOMESTIC AUTO INDUSTRY WAGE RATE TABLE
     LBSPC   - WEIGHT IN POUNDS PER CAR
     COSTPLB - COST PER POUND FOR MATERIALS (1975$/LB)
     LBST    - WEIGHT IN POUNDS PER CAR TABLE
     COSTLBT - COST PER POUND FOR MATERIALS IN AUTO TABLE
     SPCOCPC - SPECIAL COMPONENT COST (1975$/CAR)
     SPCOCPT - SPECIAL COMPONENT COST TABLE
```

DOMESTIC AUTO OUTPUT, INVENTORY, AND PRICING SECTOR

```
DAO.K=DAPC.K*DAPCUF.K*FROLOFS.K                    387, A
DAO=6E6                                            388, N
DAPCUF.K=TABXT(DAPCUFT,DAINVCR.K/INSRN,0.7,1.7,.1)* 389, A
   NCUF
DAINVCR.K=(DNAINV.K/(NDCPR.JK+1))                  390, A
DAPCUFT=1.18/1.18/1.15/1.12/1.05/.9/.8/.75/.7/.65/ 391, T
   .65
INSRN=1.0                                          392, C
NCUF=.86                                           393, C
FROLOFS.K=1-STEP(0.1,1969.8)+STEP(0.1,1970.3)      394, A
```
      DAO   - DOMESTIC AUTO OUTPUT (CARS/YEAR)
      DAPC   - DOMESTIC AUTO INDUSTRY PRODUCTION CAPACITY
                  (CARS/YEAR)
      DAPCUF - DOMESTIC AUTO PRODUCTION CAPACITY
                  UTILIZATION FACTOR
      FROLOFS- FRACTION OF OUTPUT LOST FROM LABOR STRIKES
                  (FRACTION/YR)
      DAPCUFT- DOMESTIC AUTO PRODUCTION CAPCITY
                  UTILIZATION TABLE
      DAINVCR- DOMESTIC NEW AUTO INVENTORY COVERAGE RATIO
                  (YEARS)
      INSRN - INVENTORY TO SALES RATIO NORMAL (YEARS)
      NCUF   - NORMAL CAPACITY UTILIZATION FACTOR
      DNAINV - DOMESIC NEW AUTO INVENTORY (CARS)
      NDCPR - NEW DOMESTIC CAR PURCHASE RATE (UNIT
                  ORDERS/YEAR)

DOMESTIC NEW CAR INVENTORIES

```
DNAINV.K=DNAINV.J+(DT)(DNCO.JK-DNCSR.JK)           398, L
DNAINV=6E6                                         399, N
DNCO.KL=DAO.K                                      400, R
DNCO=6E6                                           401, N
DNCSR.KL=MIN(DNAINV.K,DNCOBL.K)                    402, R
DNCOBL.K=DNCOBL.J+(DT)(NDCPR.JK-DNCSR.JK)          403, L
DNCOBL=6E6                                         404, N
```
      DNAINV - DOMESIC NEW AUTO INVENTORY (CARS)
      DNCO   - DOMESTIC NEW CAR ORDERS (CARS/YEAR)
      DNCSR - DOMESTIC NEW CAR SALES RATE (CARS/YEAR)
      DAO   - DOMESTIC AUTO OUTPUT (CARS/YEAR)
      DNCOBL - DOMESTIC NEW CAR ORDER BACKLOG (CARS)
      NDCPR - NEW DOMESTIC CAR PURCHASE RATE (UNIT
                  ORDERS/YEAR)

DOMESTIC NEW CAR PRICE

```
FPDC.K=FCSTDC.K*AMKP*FPMFI.K                          408, A
AMKP=1.32                                             409, C
FCSTDC.K=(DAILC.K+DAICC.K+DAIMC.K+SPCOMC.K)/DAO.K     410, A
FPMFI.K=TABHL(FPMFIT,DAINVCR.K/INSRN,0,2,.2)          411, A
FPMFIT=1.05/1.05/1.02/1.01/1.005/1/.99/.96/.94/.94/   412, T
.94
PPDC.K=FPDC.K*ADMKP*(1-AUTOTXC.K)                     413, A
AUTOTXC.K=STEP(1,AUTOPYR)*TXC-STEP(1,AUTOPYR+TXDUR)   414, A
*TXC
TXC=0.1                                               415, C
AUTOPYR=2100                                          416, C
TXDUR=5                                               417, C
ADMKP=1.21                                            418, C
GOVTCOS.K=AUTOTXC.K*FPDC.K*ADMKP*DNCSR.JK             419, A
     FPDC    - FACTORY PRICE OF DOMESTIC CARS (1975$/CAR)
     FCSTDC  - FACTORY COST OF DOMESTIC CARS (1975$/CAR)
     AMKP    - AVERAGE MARKUP AT FACTORY (FRACTION)
     FPMFI   - FACTORY PRICE MULTIPLIER FROM INVENTORY
               LEVEL
     DAILC   - DOMESTIC AUTO INDUSTRY LABOR COSTS
               (1975$/YEAR)
     DAICC   - DOMESTIC AUTO INDUSTRY CAPITAL COSTS
               (1975$/YR)
     DAIMC   - DOMESTIC AUTO INDUSTRY MATERIAL COSTS
               (1975$/YEAR)
     SPCOMC  - SPECIAL COMPONENT COST FOR INDUSTRY
               (1975$/YEAR)
     DAO     - DOMESTIC AUTO OUTPUT (CARS/YEAR)
     FPMFIT  - FACTORY PRICE MULTIPLIER TABLE
     DAINVCR- DOMESTIC NEW AUTO INVENTORY COVERAGE RATIO
               (YEARS)
     INSRN   - INVENTORY TO SALES RATIO NORMAL (YEARS)
     PPDC    - PURCHASE PRICE OF DOMESTIC CARS IN RETAIL
               (1975$/CAR)
     ADMKP   - AVERAGE DEALER MARKUP (FRACTION)
     AUTOTXC- PERSONAL TAX-CREDIT FRACTION
     AUTOPYR- PERSONAL TAX-CREDIT POLICY START YEAR
     TXC     - TAX CREDIT AS PERCENT OF PRICE
     TXDUR   - DURATION OF TAX CREDIT (YEARS)
     GOVTCOS- GOVERNMENT COSTS FROM PERSONAL TAX-
               CREDIT(1975 DOLLARS)
     DNCSR   - DOMESTIC NEW CAR SALES RATE (CARS/YEAR)
```

MPG OF NEW DOMESTIC CARS

```
MPGNDC.K=MPGNDC.J+(DT)(MPGNDCA.JK-MPGNDCB.JK)         423, L
MPGNDC=15.5                                          424, N
MPGNDCA.KL=MPGNDC1.K                                 425, R
MPGNDC1.K=MAX(PNCMPG.K,RNCMPG.K)                     426, A
RNCMPG.K=CLIP(RNCMPG1.K,RNCMPG2.K,TIME.K,RMPGYR)     427, A
RMPGYR=1975                                          428, C
RNCMPG1.K=TABHL(RNCMPT,TIME.K,1975,2000,5)           429, A
RNCMPT=15/20/27.5/27.5/27.5/27.5                     430, T
RNCMPG2.K=0                                          431, A
PNCMPG.K=CLIP(PNCMPG1.K,(LBS60*MPG60)/LBSPC.K,       432, A
   TIME.K,1980)
MPG60=15.5                                           433, C
LBS60=3500                                           434, C
PNCMPG1.K=X*MPGNFC.K+(1-X)*(MPGNDC.K)                435, A
X=0.5                                                436, C
MPGNDCB.KL=MPGNDC.K                                  437, R
```
        MPGNDC - MPG OF NEW DOMESTIC CARS
        MPGNDCA- MPG OF NEW DOMESTIC CARS - INCREASE RATE
        MPGNDCB- MPG OF NEW DOMESTIC CARS - DECREASE RATE
        MPGNDC1- INCREASE IN MPG (MAX(PLANNED,REGULATED))
        PNCMPG - PLANNED NEW CAR MPG-HISTORICAL PATTERN
        RNCMPG - REGULATED NEW CAR MPG
        RNCMPG1- REGULATD MPG AFTER 1975
        RNCMPG2- REGULATED MPG BEFORE 1975
        TIME   - SIMULATION TIME IN YEARS
        RMPGYR - MPG REGULATION POLICY YEAR
        RNCMPT - REGULATED MPG SCHEDULE TABLE
        PNCMPG1- PLANNED NEW CAR MPG-USING IMPORTS AS TARGET
        LBS60 - WEIGHT IN POUNDS OF NEW CARS IN 1960
        MPG60 - MPG OF NEW CARS IN 1960
        LBSPC - WEIGHT IN POUNDS PER CAR
        X   - WEIGHT ASSIGNED TO IMPORTS IN SELECTING
                   TARGET MPG
        MPGNFC - MPG OF NEW FOREIGN CARS

FOREIGN CAR PURCHASE PRICE

```
PPFC.K=TABHL(PPFCT,TIME.K,1960,2000,5)*ITARIFR.K*    444, A
  FCPMFQ.K*1E3
PPFCT=3.5/3.6/3.8/4.4/5/5.5/6/6/6                    445, T
ITARIFR.K=CLIP(ITAR1,ITAR2,TIME.K,TARYR)            446, A
TARYR=2100                                           447, C
ITAR1=1.05                                           448, C
ITAR2=1                                              449, C
FCPMFQ.K=TABHL(FCPMFQT,SFCPRI.K,0,2,0.5)            450, A
FCPMFQT=1/1/1/1.2/1.5                               451, T
SFCPRI.K=SMOOTH(FCPR1.K/FCPR2.K,1)                  452, A
SFCPRI=1                                            453, N
```
       PPFC   - PURCHASE PRICE OF FOREIGN CARS IN RETAIL
                 (1975$/CAR)
       PPFCT   - PURCHASE PRICE OF FOREIGN CARS TABLE
       TIME   - SIMULATION TIME IN YEARS
       ITARIFR- TARIFF ON FOREIGN CARS AS FRACTION OF PRICE
       FCPMFQ - FOREIGN CAR PRICE MULTIPLIER FROM IMPORT
                 QUOTA
       ITAR1   - TARIFF ON FOREIGN CARS AS FRACTION OF
                 PRICE-POLICY VARIABLE
       ITAR2   - DEFAULT TARIFF RATE
       TARYR   - YEAR TARIFF ON FOREIGN CARS BEGINS
       FCPMFQT- FOREIGN CAR PRICE MULTIPLIER FROM IMPORT
                 QUOTA TABLE
       SFCPRI - SMOOTHED RATIO OF NON-QUOTA TO QUOTA
                 FOREIGN CAR SALES
       FCPR1   - FOREIGN CAR PURCHASE RATE WITH QUOTAS
                 (CARS/YEAR)
       FCPR2   - FOREIGN CAR PURCHASE RATE WITHOUT QUOTAS
                 (CARS/YEAR)

MPG OF NEW FOREIGN CAR

```
MPGNFC.K=TABHL(MPGNFCT,TIME.K,1960,2000,5)          457, A
MPGNFCT=18/18/20/25/30/35/40/40/40                  458, T
```
       MPGNFC - MPG OF NEW FOREIGN CARS
       MPGNFCT- MPG OF NEW FOREIGN CARS TABLE
       TIME   - SIMULATION TIME IN YEARS

SUPPLEMENTARY VARIABLES

```
AIEMP.K=DAILE.K/AMHPY                              462, A
AMHPY=2000                                         463, C
PPFCX.K=PPFC.K*CONV80                              464, A
PPDCX.K=PPDC.K*CONV80                              465, A
GOVTCOSX.K=GOVTCOS.K*CONV80                        466, A
ACDCX.K=ACDC.K*CONV80                              467, A
ACFCX.K=ACFC.K*CONV80                              468, A
GASPRX.K=GASP.K*CONV80                             469, A
RPCDIX.K=RPCDI.K*CONV80                            470, A
CONV80=1.4                                         471, C
```

```
     AIEMP   - AUTO INDUSTRY EMPLOYMENT (PERSONS)
     DAILE   - DOMESTIC AUTO INDUSTRY LABOR EMPLOYED (MAN-
               HOURS/YR)
     AMHPY   - AVERAGE MAN-HOURS PER YEAR PER WORKER
     PPFCX   - PURCHASE PRICE OF FOREIGN CARS IN RETAIL
               (1980$/CAR)
     PPFC    - PURCHASE PRICE OF FOREIGN CARS IN RETAIL
               (1975$/CAR)
     CONV80  - CONVERSION FACTOR FOR 1975 TO 1980 DOLLARS
     PPDCX   - PURCHASE PRICE OF DOMESTIC CARS IN RETAIL
               (1980$/CAR)
     PPDC    - PURCHASE PRICE OF DOMESTIC CARS IN RETAIL
               (1975$/CAR)
             - GOVERNMENT COSTS FROM PERSONAL TAX-
      *        CREDIT(1980 DOLLARS)
     GOVTCOS- GOVERNMENT COSTS FROM PERSONAL TAX-
               CREDIT(1975 DOLLARS)
     ACDCX   - ANNUALIZED COST OF DOMESTIC CARS (1980$/YR/
               CAR)
     ACDC    - ANNUALIZED COST OF DOMESTIC CARS (1975$/YR/
               CAR)
     ACFCX   - ANNUALIZED COST OF FOREIGN CARS (1980$/YR/
               CAR)
     ACFC    - ANNUALIZED COST OF FOREIGN CARS (1975$/YR/
               CAR)
     GASPRX  - GASOLINE PRICE IN 1980 DOLLARS
               (1980$/GALLON)
     GASP    - GASOLINE PRICE (1975$/GALLON)
     RPCDIX  - REAL PER CAPITA DISPOSABLE INCOME IN 1980
               DOLLARS (1980$/YR)
     RPCDI   - REAL PER CAPITA DISPOSABLE INCOME
               (1975$/YEAR)
```

SPECIFICATION FOR OUTPUT

```
SPEC  DT=0.1/LENGTH=0/PLTPER=0.5                   475
     LENGTH - LENGTH OF SIMULATION PERIOD
     PLTPER - PLOT PERIOD
```

```
PRTPER.K=STEP(PRTP,PRTYR)                        476, A
PRTP=1                                           477, C
PRTYR=1960                                       478, C
TIME=1960                                        479, N
```
    PRTPER - PRINT PERIOD
    PRTP   - PRINT PERIOD SPECIFICATION CONSTANT
    PRTYR - SPECIFICATION YEAR TO BEGIN PRINTING
             RESULTS
    TIME   - SIMULATION TIME IN YEARS

  PRINT AND PLOT STATEMENTS

```
PRINT TDNC,TCIU,PPFCX,PPDCX,NDCPR,AFCMF,AIEMP,        483
  TGASCO,GSTXREV,ACDCX,ACFCX
```
    TDNC   - TOTAL DEMAND FOR NEW CARS (CARS/YEAR)
    TCIU   - TOTAL CARS IN USE (CARS)
    PPFCX - PURCHASE PRICE OF FOREIGN CARS IN RETAIL
             (1980$/CAR)
    PPDCX - PURCHASE PRICE OF DOMESTIC CARS IN RETAIL
             (1980$/CAR)
    NDCPR - NEW DOMESTIC CAR PURCHASE RATE (UNIT
             ORDERS/YEAR)
    AFCMF - ACTUAL FOREIGN CAR MARKET SHARE FRACTION
             (FRACTION)
    AIEMP - AUTO INDUSTRY EMPLOYMENT (PERSONS)
    TGASCO - TOTAL GASOLINE CONSUMED (GALLONS/YEAR)
    GSTXREV- GAS-TAX REVENUES TO GOVERNMENT (1975$)
    ACDCX - ANNUALIZED COST OF DOMESTIC CARS (1980$/YR/
             CAR)
    ACFCX - ANNUALIZED COST OF FOREIGN CARS (1980$/YR/
             CAR)

PLOT NDCPR=D,TDNC=T(0,20E6)/AFCMF=%(0,1)/VMPRD=   485
  V(0,10E3)
```
    NDCPR  - NEW DOMESTIC CAR PURCHASE RATE (UNIT
             ORDERS/YEAR)
    TDNC   - TOTAL DEMAND FOR NEW CARS (CARS/YEAR)
    AFCMF  - ACTUAL FOREIGN CAR MARKET SHARE FRACTION
             (FRACTION)

```
PLOT POP=P,LD=L(0,300E6)/TCIU=*(0,150E6)/TVMT=T(0, 486
  2000E9)
```
    POP    - US POPULATION (PERSONS)
    LD     - NUMBER OF LICENSED DRIVERS
    TCIU   - TOTAL CARS IN USE (CARS)

```
PLOT AMTPV=M(0,20E3)/TQUAGC=Q(0,20)/GASPRX=G(0,4)/ 487
  ALC=A(0,16)
```
    AMTPV  - AVG MILES TRAVELLED PER VEHICLE (MILES/
             YEAR)
    TQUAGC - TOTAL QUADS OF GASOLINE CONSUMED (QUADS/
             YEAR)
    GASPRX - GASOLINE PRICE IN 1980 DOLLARS
             (1980$/GALLON)
    ALC    - AVG LIFE OF CAR (YEARS)

161
```

AUTO1 MODEL VARIABLES AND THEIR DEFINITIONS

```
A          CONSTANT TERM IN VMPRD EQUATION
AAAC       AVERAGE AGE OF ALL CARS ON THE ROAD (YEARS)
AADC       AVERAGE AGE OF DOMESTIC CARS ON THE ROAD (YEARS)
AADCCR     AVERAGE AGE OF DOMESTIC CARS CHANGE RATE
AADC1      AN INTERMEDIATE AUXILLARY VARIABLE
AAFC       AVERAGE AGE OF FOREIGN CARS ON THE ROAD (YEARS)
AAFCCR     AVERAGE AGE OF FOREIGN CARS CHANGE RATE
AAFC1      AN INTERMEDIATE AUXILLARY VARIABLE
AAUCI      AVERAGE AGE OF USED CARS IN INVENTORY (YEARS)
AAUCIR     AVERAGE AGE OF USED CARS IN INVENTORY CHANGE RATE
AAUC1      AN INTERMEDIATE AUXILLARY VARIABLE
ACDC       ANNUALIZED COST OF DOMESTIC CARS (1975$/YR/CAR)
ACDCX      ANNUALIZED COST OF DOMESTIC CARS (1980$/YR/CAR)
ACDEPYR    ACCELERATED DEPRECIATION POLICY YEAR
ACDT       ACCELERATED DEPRECIATION POLICY DURATION (YEARS)
ACFC       ANNUALIZED COST OF FOREIGN CARS (1975$/YR/CAR)
ACFCX      ANNUALIZED COST OF FOREIGN CARS (1980$/YR/CAR)
ACNC       AVERAGE ANNUALIZED COST OF NEW CARS (1975$/YR/CAR)
ACTID      ACCELERATED TRADEIN POLICY DURATION (YEARS)
ACTIPYR    ACCELERATED TRADEIN POLICY YEAR
ACUDC      ANNUALIZED COST OF USED DOMESTIC CARS (1975$/YR/CAR)
ADMKP      AVERAGE DEALER MARKUP (FRACTION)
AFCMF      ACTUAL FOREIGN CAR MARKET SHARE FRACTION (FRACTION)
AIEMP      AUTO INDUSTRY EMPLOYMENT (PERSONS)
ALC        AVG LIFE OF CAR (YEARS)
ALCT       AVERAGE LIFE OF CAR TABLE
ALCN       AVERAGE LIFE OF CAR NORMAL (YEARS)
ALDAPC     AVG LIFETIME OF DOMESTIC AUTO PRODUCTION CAPACITY (YEARS)
ALP        INCOME ELASTICITY PARAMETER FOR VMPRD
AMHPA      AVERAGE MAN-HOURS PER AUTO PRODUCTION (MAN-HOURS/CAR)
AMHPAT     AVG. MAN HOURS PER AUTO TABLE
AMHPY      AVERAGE MAN-HOURS PER YEAR PER WORKER
AMKP       AVERAGE MARKUP AT FACTORY (FRACTION)
AMPGAC     AVERAGE MPG OF ALL CARS ON THE ROAD
AMPGDC     AVG MPG OF DOMESTIC CARS IN USE
AMPGDCR    AVG MPG OF DOMESTIC CARS - CHANGE RATE
AMPGFC     AVG MPG OF FOREIGN CARS IN USE
AMPGFCR    AVG MPG OF FOREIGN CARS - CHANGE RATE
AMPGUCR    AVG MPG OF USED DOMESTIC CARS - CHANGE RATE
AMPGUDC    AVG MPG OF USED DOMESTIC CARS
AMTPV      AVG MILES TRAVELLED PER VEHICLE (MILES/YEAR)
AMTPVN     AVG MILES TRAVELLED PER VEHICLE NORMAL (MILES/YEAR)
APUDC      AVG PRICE OF USED DOMESTIC CAR (1975$/CAR)
ARROS      AVG RATE OF RETURN ON SALES (FRACTION/YEAR)
AUSC       AUTO USE SMOOTHING CONSTANT (YEARS)
AUTOPYR    PERSONAL TAX-CREDIT POLICY START YEAR
AUTOTXC    PERSONAL TAX-CREDIT FRACTION
BET        PRICE ELASTICITY PARAMETER FOR VMPRD
CAPISC     CAPACITY UTILIZATION INVEST.MULTIPLIER SMOOTHING CONST (YRS)
CMF        CURRENT MARKET FRACTION OF FOREIGN CARS TO TOTAL CARS IN USE
```

CONST	A CONSTANT TERM IN DTSOC EQUATION
CONV80	CONVERSION FACTOR FOR 1975 TO 1980 DOLLARS
COSTLBT	COST PER POUND FOR MATERIALS IN AUTO TABLE
COSTPLB	COST PER POUND FOR MATERIALS (1975$/LB)
CX1	A CONSTANT TERM IN TDNC EQUATION
CX2	A SECOND CONSTANT TERM IN TDNC EQUATION
CX4	REAL INCOME ELASTICITY OF NEW CAR DEMAND IN TDNC EQUATION
CX5	AVERAGE ANNUALIZED NEW CAR COST ELASTICITY OF NEW CAR DEMAND IN TDNC EQUATION
CX6	NEW CAR DEMAND ELASTICITY WRT. %CHANGE IN UNEMPLOYMENT FROM FROM PREVIOUS PERIOD
DAAST	DOMESTIC AUTO INDUSTRY ASSETS (1975$)
DACCR	DOMESTIC AUTO CAPACITY COST RATIO (1975$/CAR/YEAR)
DACCRT	DOMESTIC AUTO CAPACITY COST RATIO TABLE
DAFCT	DOMESTIC AUTO AVG FACILITY CONSTRUCTION TIME (YEARS)
DAIC	DOMESTIC AUTO INDUSTRY INVESTMENT IN CAPACITY (CARS/YR/YR)
DAICC	DOMESTIC AUTO INDUSTRY CAPITAL COSTS (1975$/YR)
DAICST	DOMESTIC AUTO INDUSTRY COSTS (1975$/YR)
DAIFCR	DOMESTIC AUTO INDUSTRY FIXED CHARGE RATE (FRACTION/YEAR)
DAIIF	DOMESTIC AUTO INDUSTRY INVESTMENT FRACTION (FRACTION/YR)
DAIIFN	DOMESTIC AUTO INDUSTRY INVESTMENT FRACTION NORMAL (FRAC./YR)
DAIIFT	DOMESTIC AUTO INDUSTRY INVESTMENT FRACTION TABLE
DAILC	DOMESTIC AUTO INDUSTRY LABOR COSTS (1975$/YEAR)
DAILE	DOMESTIC AUTO INDUSTRY LABOR EMPLOYED (MAN-HOURS/YR)
DAIMC	DOMESTIC AUTO INDUSTRY MATERIAL COSTS (1975$/YEAR)
DAIMCU	DOMESTIC AUTO INVEST. MULTIPLIER FROM CAPACITY UTILIZATION
DAINVCR	DOMESTIC NEW AUTO INVENTORY COVERAGE RATIO (YEARS)
DAIWR	DOMESTIC AUTO INDUSTRY WAGE RATE (1975$/MAN HOUR)
DAIWRT	DOMESTIC AUTO INDUSTRY WAGE RATE TABLE
DAO	DOMESTIC AUTO OUTPUT (CARS/YEAR)
DAPC	DOMESTIC AUTO INDUSTRY PRODUCTION CAPACITY (CARS/YEAR)
DAPCAR	DOMESTIC AUTO PRODUCTION CAPACITY ADDITION RATE (CARS/YR/YR)
DAPCDIR	DOMESTIC AUTO PROD. CAP. DISCARD RATE (CARS/YR/YR)
DAPCDR	DOMESTIC AUTO PRODUCTION CAPACITY DEPRECIATION RATE (CARS/Y/Y)
DAPCUF	DOMESTIC AUTO PRODUCTION CAPACITY UTILIZATION FACTOR
DAPCUFT	DOMESTIC AUTO PRODUCTION CAPCITY UTILIZATION TABLE
DAPRO	DOMESTIC AUTO INDUSTRY PROFITS (1975$/YEAR)
DAREV	DOMESTIC AUTO INDUSTRY REVENUES (1975$/YEAR)
DAROS	DOMESTIC AUTO INDUSTRY RETURN ON SALES (FRACTION)
DAT	DEMAND ADJUSTMENT TIME (YEARS)
DCDISC	DOMESTIC CAPACITY DISCARD SMOOTHING CONSTANT (YEARS)
DCER	DOMESTIC CAR EARLY RETIREMENTS (CARS/YEAR)
DCER1	DOMESTIC CAR EARLY RETIREMENTS-INTERMEDIATE VARIABLE
DCETI	DOMESTIC CAR EARLY TRADEINS (CARS/YEAR)
DCIU	DOMESTIC CARS IN USE (CARS)
DCRR	DOMESTIC CAR RETIREMENT RATE (CARS/YEAR)
DFUDC	DEMAND FOR USED DOMESTIC CARS (CARS/YEAR)
DNAINV	DOMESIC NEW AUTO INVENTORY (CARS)
DNCO	DOMESTIC NEW CAR ORDERS (CARS/YEAR)
DNCOBL	DOMESTIC NEW CAR ORDER BACKLOG (CARS)

.

DNCSR	DOMESTIC NEW CAR SALES RATE (CARS/YEAR)
DOITC	TAX CREDIT FOR TRADEIN/RETIRE OLD CAR FOR NEW DOM.CARS
DOITCT	DOITC(TAX CREDIT)TABLE
DTIFDC	DEPRECIATION, TAXES, INSURANCE AS FRACTION OF INITIAL COSTS OF DOMESTIC CAR
DTIFDCC	DTIFDC CONSTANT
DTIFFC	DEPRECIATION, TAXES, INSURANCE AS FRACTION OF INITIAL COSTS OF FOREIGN CAR
DTIFFCC	DTIFFC CONSTANT
DTIFUCC	DTIFUDC CONSTANT
DTIFUDC	DEPRECIATION, TAXES, INSURANCE AS FRACTION OF INITIAL COST OF USED DOMESTIC CAR
DTSOC	DESIRED TOTAL STOCK OF CARS (CARS)
ELD	ELASTICITY WRT. LICENSED DRIVERS IN DTSOC EQUATION
FCIU	FOREIGN CARS IN USE (CARS)
FCMF	FOREIGN CAR MARKET CAPTURE FRACTION - TOTAL U.S MARKET
FCMFCR	FOREIGN CAR MARKET CAPTURE FRACTION CHANGE RATE-SMALL CAR MKT
FCMFIN	FOREIGN CAR MARKET CAPTURE FRACTION INITIAL IN 1960 -SM.CAR.MKT
FCMFSC	FOREIGN CAR MARKET CAPTURE FRACTION - U.S. SMALL CAR MKT.
FCMPD	FOREIGN CAR MARKET PENETRATION DELAY (YEARS)
FCMPDT	FOREIGN CAR MARKET PENETRATION DELAY TABLE
FCPMFQ	FOREIGN CAR PRICE MULTIPLIER FROM IMPORT QUOTA
FCPMFQT	FOREIGN CAR PRICE MULTIPLIER FROM IMPORT QUOTA TABLE
FCPR	FOREIGN CAR PURCHASE RATE (CARS/YEAR)
FCPR1	FOREIGN CAR PURCHASE RATE WITH QUOTAS (CARS/YEAR)
FCPR2	FOREIGN CAR PURCHASE RATE WITHOUT QUOTAS (CARS/YEAR)
FCRDC	FIXED CHARGE RATE FOR NEW DOMESTIC CARS (FRACTION/YR)
FCRFC	FIXED CHARGE RATE FOR FOREIGN CARS (FRACTION/YR)
FCRR	FOREIGN CAR RETIREMENT RATE (CARS/YEAR)
FCRUC	FIXED CHARGE RATE FOR USED CARS (FRACTION/YEAR)
FCSTDC	FACTORY COST OF DOMESTIC CARS (1975$/CAR)
FCWF	FOREIGN CAR WEIGHTAGE FACTOR IN ACNC EQUATION (FRACTION)
FDCRE	FRACTION OF DOMESTIC CARS RETIRED EARLY
FDCRET	FRACTION RETIRED EARLY AS FUNCTION OF TAX REBATE TABLE
FP	FINANCING PERIOD FOR NEW CARS (YEARS)
FPC	FINANCING PERIOD CONSTANT (YEARS)
FPDC	FACTORY PRICE OF DOMESTIC CARS. (1975$/CAR)
FPMFI	FACTORY PRICE MULTIPLIER FROM INVENTORY LEVEL
FPMFIT	FACTORY PRICE MULTIPLIER TABLE
FPUC	FINANCING PERIOD FOR USED CARS (YEARS)
FRACD	FRACTION OF CAPACITY DISCARDED (FRACTION/YR)
FRACDT	FRACTION OF CAPACITY DISCARDED TABLE
FROLOFS	FRACTION OF OUTPUT LOST FROM LABOR STRIKES (FRACTION/YR)
GASCDC	GASOLINE CONSUMED BY DOMESTIC CARS (GALLONS/YEAR)
GASCFC	GASOLINE CONSUMED BY FOREIGN CARS (GALLONS/YEAR)
GASP	GASOLINE PRICE (1975$/GALLON)
GASPI	GASOLINE PRICE INDEX (1975=100)
GASPIX	GASOLINE PRICE INDEX WITH TAX
GASPI1	GASOLINE PRICE INDEX 1960-1980
GASPI2	GASOLINE PRICE INDEX 1980-2000

.

GASPI1T	GASPI1 TABLE
GASPI2T	GASPI2 TABLE
GASPI75	CONVERSION FACTOR TO 1975 BASE YEAR
GASP75	GASOLINE PRICE IN 1975 (1975$/GALLON)
GASPRX	GASOLINE PRICE IN 1980 DOLLARS (1980$/GALLON)
GASTAB	GASOLINE TAX TABLE
GASTAX	GASOLINE TAX (1975$/GALLON)
GOVPD	GOVERNMENT INCENTIVE POLICY DURATION (YEARS)
GOVPYR	GOVERNMENT INCENTIVE POLICY YEARS
GOVTCOS	GOVERNMENT COSTS FROM PERSONAL TAX-CREDIT(1975 DOLLARS)
GOVTCOSX	GOVERNMENT COSTS FROM PERSONAL TAX-CREDIT(1980 DOLLARS)
GOVTINC	GOVERNMENT INCENTIVES (1975$/YEAR)
GOVYR	GOVERNMENT INCENTIVE POLICY BEGINNING YEAR
GPQ	GALLONS OF GASOLINE PER QUAD
GSHORT	FRACTION OF VMT DEMAND UNSATISFIED BY GASOLINE SHORTAGE
GSTXREV	GAS-TAX REVENUES TO GOVERNMENT (1975$)
IAQD	IMPORT QUOTA DURATION (YEARS)
IAQU	IMPORT QUOTA CARS (CARS/YEAR)
IAQY	IMPORT QUOTA BEGINNING YEAR
IE	INCOME ELASTICITY OF CAR-STOCK DEMAND
IFCMFSC	INDICATED FOREIGN CAR MARKET FRACTION-SMALL CAR MARKET
IFCMFT	INDICATED FOREIGN CAR MKT. FRACTION TABLE
INSRN	INVENTORY TO SALES RATIO NORMAL (YEARS)
INTC	INTEREST RATE INITIAL (FRACTION/YR)
INTDC	INTEREST RATE FOR FINANCING NEW DOMESTIC CARS (FRACTION/YR)
INTFC	INTEREST RATE FOR FINANCING FOREIGN CARS (FRACTION/YEAR)
INTPX	INTEREST RATE SUBSIDY POLICY RATE
INTPYR	INTEREST RATE SUBSIDY POLICY INITIATION YEAR
INTU	INTEREST RATE FOR FINANCING USED CARS (FRACTION/YR)
ITARIFR	TARIFF ON FOREIGN CARS AS FRACTION OF PRICE
ITAR1	TARIFF ON FOREIGN CARS AS FRACTION OF PRICE-POLICY VARIABLE
ITAR2	DEFAULT TARIFF RATE
LBSPC	WEIGHT IN POUNDS PER CAR
LBST	WEIGHT IN POUNDS PER CAR TABLE
LBS60	WEIGHT IN POUNDS OF NEW CARS IN 1960
LD	NUMBER OF LICENSED DRIVERS
LDFP	LICENSED DRIVERS AS A FRACTION OF POPULATION
LDFP1	LICENSED DRIVER FRACTION 1980-2000
LDFP2	LICENSED DRIVER FRACTION 1960-1980
LDFP1T	LDFP1 TABLE
LDFP2T	LDFP2 TABLE
LENGTH	LENGTH OF SIMULATION PERIOD
MPGNDC	MPG OF NEW DOMESTIC CARS
MPGNDCA	MPG OF NEW DOMESTIC CARS - INCREASE RATE
MPGNDCB	MPG OF NEW DOMESTIC CARS - DECREASE RATE
MPGNDC1	INCREASE IN MPG (MAX(PLANNED,REGULATED))
MPGNFC	MPG OF NEW FOREIGN CARS
MPGNFCT	MPG OF NEW FOREIGN CARS TABLE
MPG60	MPG OF NEW CARS IN 1960
MUDCICR	MULTIPLIER FOR USED DOMESTIC CAR INVENTORY COVERAGE

.

MUDCT	MULTIPLIER FOR USED DOMESTIC CAR INVENTORY COVERAGE TABLE
NCUCCR	NEW CAR USED CAR COST RATIO
NCUF	NORMAL CAPACITY UTILIZATION FACTOR
NDCPR	NEW DOMESTIC CAR PURCHASE RATE (UNIT ORDERS/YEAR)
NTRADIN	NORMAL TRADE-INS OF USED CARS FOR NEW DOMESTIC CARS (CARS/YR)
NTRADINF	NORMAL TRADE-INS AS A FRACTION OF DOMESTIC CARS IN USE
OAMCDC	OPERATING AND MAINTENANCE COSTS FOR DOMESTIC CAR (1975$/YEAR)
OAMCFC	OPERATING AND MAINTENANCE COSTS FOR FOREIGN CAR (1975$/YEAR)
OAMCUC	OPERATING AND MAINTENANCE COST OF USED CAR (1975$/YEAR)
OAMCUCN	OPERATING AND MAINTENANCE COST FOR USED CAR NORMAL (1975$/MI)
OAMPMDC	OPERATING AND MAINTENANCE COST PER MILE - DOMESTIC CAR (75$/MI)
OAMPMFC	OPERATING AND MAINTENANCE COST PER MILE - FOREIGN CAR (75$/MI)
OGCDC	OIL AND GAS COST FOR DOMESTIC CAR (1975$/YR/CAR)
OGCDCUC	OIL AND GAS COST FOR DOMESTIC USED CAR (1975$/YEAR/CAR)
OGCFC	OIL AND GAS COST FOR FOREIGN CAR (1975$/YEAR/CAR)
PLTPER	PLOT PERIOD
PNCMPG	PLANNED NEW CAR MPG-HISTORICAL PATTERN
PNCMPG1	PLANNED NEW CAR MPG-USING IMPORTS AS TARGET
POP	US POPULATION (PERSONS)
POP1	US POPULATION - 1980-2000
POP2	US POPULATION - 1960-1980
POP1T	POP1 TABLE
POP2T	POP2 TABLE
PPDC	PURCHASE PRICE OF DOMESTIC CARS IN RETAIL (1975$/CAR)
PPDCX	PURCHASE PRICE OF DOMESTIC CARS IN RETAIL (1980$/CAR)
PPFC	PURCHASE PRICE OF FOREIGN CARS IN RETAIL (1975$/CAR)
PPFCT	PURCHASE PRICE OF FOREIGN CARS TABLE
PPFCX	PURCHASE PRICE OF FOREIGN CARS IN RETAIL (1980$/CAR)
PRTP	PRINT PERIOD SPECIFICATION CONSTANT
PRTPER	PRINT PERIOD
PRTYR	SPECIFICATION YEAR TO BEGIN PRINTING RESULTS
RAUDCI	RATE OF ADDITIONS TO USED DOMESTIC CAR INVENTORIES (CARS/YR)
RIPI75	CONVERSION FACTOR FROM 1972 TO 1975 DOLLARS
RMPGYR	MPG REGULATION POLICY YEAR
RNCMPG	REGULATED NEW CAR MPG
RNCMPG1	REGULATD MPG AFTER 1975
RNCMPG2	REGULATED MPG BEFORE 1975
RNCMPT	REGULATED MPG SCHEDULE TABLE
ROSSC	RETURN ON SALES SMOOTHING CONSTANT (YEARS)
RPCDI	REAL PER CAPITA DISPOSABLE INCOME (1975$/YEAR)
RPCDIX	REAL PER-CAPITA DISPOSABLE INCOME IN 1980 DOLLARS (1980$/YR)
RPCDI1	REAL PER-CAPITA DISPOSABLE INCOME 1960-1980
RPCDI2	REAL PER CAPITA DISPOSABLE INCOME 1980-2000
RPCDI1T	RPCDI1 TABLE
RPCDI2T	RPCDI2 TABLE
SAFCMF	SMOOTHED ACTUAL FOREIGN CAR MARKET SHARE FRACTION
SAMTPV	SMOOTHED AVERAGE MILES TRAVELED PER VEHICLE (MILES/YEAR)
SCMSF	SMALL CAR MARKET SHARE FRACTION OF TOTAL U.S. MARKET
SCMSFT	SMALL CAR MARKET SHARE TABLE
SD	DURATION OF GASOLINE SHORTAGE (YEARS)

.

SDAPCUF	SMOOTHED DOMESTIC AUTO PROD. CAPACITY UTIL. FACTOR
SF	FRACTION OF GASOLINE DEMAND UNSATISFIED FROM SHORTAGE
SFCPRI	SMOOTHED RATIO OF NON-QUOTA TO QUOTA FOREIGN CAR SALES
SFDACR	SMOOTHED FOREIGN TO DOMESTIC CAR ANNUALIZED COST RATIO
SPCOCPC	SPECIAL COMPONENT COST (1975$/CAR)
SPCOCPT	SPECIAL COMPONENT COST TABLE
SPCOMC	SPECIAL COMPONENT COST FOR INDUSTRY (1975$/YEAR)
SPEC	OUPUT SPECIFICATIONS
SRROS	SMOOTHED RATE OF RETURN ON SALES (FRACTION/YEAR)
SYR	GASOLINE SHORTAGE YEAR
TARYR	YEAR TARIFF ON FOREIGN CARS BEGINS
TCIU	TOTAL CARS IN USE (CARS)
TCQUAC	TOTAL CUMULATIVE QUADS CONSUMED (QUADS)
TCQUACR	TOTAL CUMULATIVE QUADS CONSUMED - CHANGE RATE
TDNC	TOTAL DEMAND FOR NEW CARS (CARS/YEAR)
TGASCO	TOTAL GASOLINE CONSUMED (GALLONS/YEAR)
TIME	SIMULATION TIME IN YEARS
TQUAGC	TOTAL QUADS OF GASOLINE CONSUMED (QUADS/YEAR)
TRADT	TRADE-IN FRACTION TABLE
TRET	TOTAL RETIREMENTS (SCRAP) OF CARS (CARS/YEAR)
TVMT	TOTAL VEHICLE MILES TRAVELLED BY CARS (MILES/YEAR)
TXC	TAX CREDIT AS PERCENT OF PRICE
TXDUR	DURATION OF TAX CREDIT (YEARS)
UCINCN	USED CAR INVENTORY COVERAGE NORMAL (YEARS)
UCMF	USED CAR MARKET FRACTION
UCMFT	USED CAR MARKET FRACTION TABLE
UCNCUR	USED CAR NORMAL USAGE RATE AS A FRACTION OF NEW CAR USE
UDCI	USED DOMESTIC CAR INVENTORY (CARS)
UDCPR	USED DOMESTIC CAR PURCHASE RATE (CARS/YEAR)
UDCPX	USED DOMESTIC CAR INTERMEDIATE AUXILLIARY VARIABLE (CARS/YR)
URPCPY	UNEMPLOYMENT RATE PERCENT CHANGE FROM PREVIOUS YR.(%)
URPCPY1	UNEMPLOYMENT RATE PERCENT CHANGE FROM PREV.YR, 1980-90
URPCPY2	UNEMPLOYMENT RATE PERCENT CHANGE FROM PREV.YR, 1960-80
URPCT1	URPCPY1 TABLE
URPCT2	URPCPY2 TABLE
VMPRD	VEHICLE MILES PER REGISTERED DRIVER (MILES/DRIVER/YEAR)
X	WEIGHT ASSIGNED TO IMPORTED CAR MPG IN SELECTING TARGET MPG FOR NEW DOMESTIC CAR

EXECUTION RUN CARDS

THE FOLLOWING STATEMENTS WILL EXECUTE THE BASE CASE RUN AND
THE POLICIES TESTED IN THE FOURTH CHAPTER OF THIS BOOK. THE MODEL
USER MAY WISH TO TEST ANY OTHER POLICIES SUCH AS ACCELERATED TRADE-
IN OR ACCELERATED RETIREMENTS, INDUSTRY DIRECT SUBSIDIES, AND MPG
REGULATIONS , AND SO ON.

```
RUN
C      IAQY=1981.4
C      IAQD=2
C      IAQU=2.2E6
CP     LENGTH=1990
CP     PLTPER=1
C      PRTYR=1960
RUN BASE CASE
CP     PRTYR=1980
RUN BASE CASE WITHOUT QUOTA
C      IAQD=9
C      IAQU=2E6
C      IAQY=1981.4
RUN 2MIL. QUOTA FROM 1981.4 TO 1990
C      IAQD=9
C      IAQU=1E6
C      IAQY=1981.4
RUN 1 MILL. QUOTA FROM 1981.4 TO 1990
CP     IAQY=1981.4
CP     IAQD=2
CP     IAQU=2.2E6
T      DAIWRT=6.8/7.3/8/9.5/11/11/11/11/11
RUN CONST 1980 REAL WAGES TO 1990
T      DAIWRT=6.8/7.3/8/9.5/11/8.25/8.25/8.25/8.25
RUN 30% DECLINE IN REAL WAGE RATE BY 85 THEN CONST
T      DAIWRT=6.8/7.3/8/9.5/11/5.5/5.5/5.5/5.5
RUN 50% DECLINE IN REAL WAGE RATE BY 1985 THEN CONST.
T      AMHPAT=235/192/179/143/140/100/90/80/80
RUN 40 PERCENT INCREASE IN PRODUCTIVITY BY 1985 AND 20% MORE BY 1990
T      GASTAB=0/0/0.5/.5/.5/.5/.5/.5/.5/.5/.5/.5/.5/.5/.5/
X      .5/.5/.5/.5/.5
RUN 50 CENT GAS TAX 1983-1990
T      GASTAB=0/0/0.1/.1/.1/.1/.1/.1/.1/.1/.1/.1/.1/.1/.1/
X      .1/.1/.1/.1/.1
RUN 10 CENT GAS TAX FROM 1983
C      TXDUR=1
C      AUTOPYR=1981.9
RUN 10% PERSONAL TAX CREDIT FOR ONE YEAR
TP     RPCDI2T=4.567/4.57/4.88/5.17/5.49/5.83/5.83/5.83/5.83/5.83/5.83
RUN 3% PER YR. INCOME GROWTH AFTER 1982
C      TXDUR=1
C      AUTOPYR=1981.9
RUN 10% PERSONAL TAX-CREDIT UNDER HIGH GROWTH
TP     RPCDI2T=4.567/4.57/4.6/4.6/4.6/4.6/4.6/4.6/4.6/4.6
RUN BASE CASE W/ZERO INCOME GROWTH
C      TXDUR=1
C      AUTOPYR=1981.9
RUN 10% PERSONAL TAX CREDIT UNDER ZERO GROWTH
```

Bibliography

Abernathy, William J., Kim B. Clark, and Alan M. Kantrow. 1981. "The New Industrial Competition." *Harvard Business Review*, Sept./Oct. 1981, vol. 59, no. 5. Boston, Mass.: Harvard University.

Allen, Edward L., and James A. Edmonds. 1979. *The Future of the Personal Automobile in the United States*. Institute for Energy Analysis. ORAU/IEA-79-14(M), Research Memorandum. Oak Ridge Associated Universities.

Argyris, Chris. 1964. *Integrating the Individual and the Organization*. New York: John Wiley and Sons.

Auto Hearings. 1981. See U.S. Congress, Senate. Committee on Commerce, Science and Transportation.

Automotive News. Various issues, weekly publication. Detroit.

Automotive News. Annual volumes 1975-80. Almanac Issue. Detroit.

Automotive Testing Laboratories. 1979. *A Study of Emissions from Passenger Cars in Six Cities*. Prepared for the U.S. Environmental Protection Agency. January 1979.

Chase Econometrics. 1974. *The Effect of Tax and Regulatory Alternatives on Car Sales and Gasoline Consumption*. New York, New York.

Chow, G. C. 1957. *Demand for Automobiles in the United States*. Amsterdam: North Holland.

Chrysler. 1981. *Report to Shareholders for the Year Ended December 31, 1980*. Detroit.

Consumers Union. 1981. "Frequency-of-Repair Records, 1975-1980." *Consumers Report*. April 1981, pp. 225-235.

Comptroller General. 1979. *United States-Japan Trade: Issues and Problems.* ID-79-53. Washington, D.C.: General Accounting Office.

Council of Economic Advisors. 1981. *Economic Report of the President 1981.* Washington, D.C.: Government Printing Office.

———. 1980. *Economic Report of the President 1980.* Washington, D.C.: Government Printing Office.

Crandall, Robert W., and Lester B. Lave. 1981. *The Scientific Basis of Health and Safety Regulation.* Washington, D.C.: The Brookings Institution.

Dahlman, Carl. 1979. "The Problem of Externalities." *Journal of Law and Economics*, April 1979, vol. XX21 (1), p. 141.

Drucker, Peter F. 1974. *Management: Tasks, Responsibilities, Practices.* New York: Harper and Row.

Editors of Consumer Guide. 1981. *Used Car Rating and Price Guide.* 1971-80. New York City: Galahad Books.

Energy and Environmental Analysis, Inc. 1975. *Gasoline Consumption Model.* Washington, D.C.: Federal Energy Administration.

Environmental Protection Agency. 1980. *Passenger Car and Light Truck Fuel Economy Trends Through 1980.* SAE Technical Paper Series 800853. Warrendale, Pa.: Society of Automotive Engineers, Inc.

Euro Finance. 1980. *European Car Industry Report.* Number 4.

Far Eastern Economic Review. 1981. February 27, 1981, Issue. Hong Kong.

Fearnsides, J. J. et al. 1980. *The U.S. Transportation System: An Overview.* MTR-80W162. McLean, Va.: The MITRE Corporation.

Federal Task Force. 1976. *The Report by the Federal Task Force on Motor Vehicle Goals Beyond 1980.* U.S. Department of Transportation. Washington, D.C. September 1976.

Flaim, Paul O., and Howard N. Fullerton. 1978. "Labor Force Projections to 1990 – Three Possible Paths." *Monthly Labor Review.* December 1978. U.S. Department of Labor, Bureau of Labor Statistics. pp. 25-35.

Ford Motor Company. 1981a. *Ford Annual Report 1980.* Detroit.

_____ . 1981b. *Annual Report on Form 10-K for the Year Ended December 31, 1980*. Detroit.

Freeman III, A. M., Robert H. Haveman, and Allan V. Kneese. 1973. *The Economics of Environmental Policy*. New York: John Wiley and Sons.

General Motors. 1981a. *Annual Report 1980*. Detroit.

_____ . 1981b. *General Motors Public Interest Report*. Detroit.

_____ . 1981c. Press Release. Detroit. September 14.

Ginzberg, Eli, and George J. Vojta. 1981. "The Service Sector of the U.S. Economy." *Scientific American*. March 1981, vol. 244, pp. 48-55.

Gray, Charles L., and Frank von Hippel. 1981. "The Fuel Economy of Light Vehicles." *Scientific American*. May 1981, vol. 244, pp. 48-59.

Greene, David L. 1981. *Aggregate Demand for Gasoline and Highway Passenger Vehicles in the United States: A Review of the Literature 1938-1978*. ORNL-5728. Oak Ridge, Tenn.: Oak Ridge National Laboratory. July 1981.

Harberger, Arnold C., ed. 1960. *Demand for Durable Goods*. Chicago: University of Chicago Press.

Harbour, James E. 1981. *Comparison and Analysis of Automotive Manufacturing Productivity in the Japanese and North American Automotive Industries for the Manufacture of Subcompact and Compact Cars*. Berkeley, Mich.: Harbour and Associates, Inc.

Henderson, James M., and Richard E. Quandt. 1971. *Microeconomic Theory — A Mathematical Approach*, 2d ed. New York: McGraw Hill.

Hess, Alan C. 1977. "A Comparison of Automobile Demand Equations." *Econometrica*. vol. 45, no. 3., pp. 683-701.

International Labour Office. 1977. *Labour Force Estimates and Projection 1950-2000*. 2d ed. Geneva, Switzerland.

J. D. Power and Associates. 1981. *The Power Newsletter*. June 1981, vol. 5, no. 4. Los Angeles.

Kannan, N. P. 1981. "The Access Theory of Demand." Working Paper #5. Arlington, Va.: Kannan and Associates.

Kannan, N.·P., K. K. Rebibo, and D. L. Ellis. 1981. *Fuel Efficiency of Passenger Cars and the Domestic Auto Industry.* MTR-81W104. McLean, Va.: The MITRE Corporation. May 1981.

Lave, Lester B. 1981. "Conflicting Objectives in Regulating the Automobile." *Science.* vol. 216, pp. 893-899.

MacGregor, Douglas. 1960. *The Human Side of Interprise.* New York: McGraw Hill.

Maslow, A. H. 1954. *Motivation and Personality.* New York: Harper and Row.

Mills, Edwin S., and Lawrence J. White. 1978. "Auto Emissions: Why Regulation Hasn't Worked." *Technology Review.* March/April 1978, pp. 54-63.

Motor Vehicle Manufacturers Association. 1981. *Facts and Figures '81.* Detroit.

_____. 1980. *Facts and Figures '80.* Detroit.

Nash, Carl E. 1981. "A Regulator's View." *The Scientific Basis of Health and Safety Regulation.* Edited by Robert W. Crandall and Lester B. Lave, pp. 53-67. Washington, D.C.: The Brookings Institution.

National Automobile Dealers Association. 1981. *NADA Data for 1981.* McLean, Va.

National Safety Council. 1981. *Accident Facts.* Chicago.

Nerlove, Marc. 1957. "A Note on Long Run Automobile Demand." *Journal of Marketing.* July 1957, pp. 57-64.

Office of Technology Assessment. 1981. *U.S. Industrial Competitiveness – A Comparison of Steel, Electronics, and Automobiles.* Washington, D.C.: Congress of the United States.

Organization for Economic Cooperation and Development. 1980. Statistical Reports. Paris.

Ouchi, William G. 1981. *Theory Z.* New York: Avon Books.

Paine Webber. Various Issues. *Car and Truck Monthly Report.* New York: Paine Webber Mitchell Hutchins, Inc.

Pascale, Richard T., and Anthony G. Athos. 1981. *The Art of Japanese Management: Application for American Executives*. New York: Warner Books.

Phillips, Benjamin. 1980. *Safety Belt Usage Among Drivers*. Opinion Research Corporation for the National Highway Traffic Safety Administration. DOT-HS-805-398. May 1980.

Pigou, A. C. 1946. *The Economics of Welfare*. 4th ed. London: MacMillan.

Pugh, Alexander L. 1977. *DYNAMO User's Manual*. 5th ed. Cambridge, Mass.: The MIT Press.

Rebibo, K., G. Bennington, P. Curto, P. Spewak, and R. Vitray. 1977. *A System for Projecting the Utilization of Renewable Resources – SPURR Methodology*. MTR-7570. McLean, Va.: The MITRE Corporation.

Schuessler, Robert, and Rene Smith. 1974. *Working Models of Fuel Consumption, Emissions, and Safety Related to Auto Usage and Purchasing Behavior*. Working Paper WP-23-U2-52. Transportation Systems Center. Cambridge, Mass.

Schumpeter, Joseph. 1942. *Capitalism, Socialism, and Democracy*. New York: Harper Brothers.

Shackson, Richard H., and James H. Leach. 1980. *Using Fuel Economy and Synthetic Fuels to Compete with OPEC Oil*. The Energy Productivity Center. Arlington, Va.: Mellon Institute.

Smith, R. P. 1975. *Consumer Demand for Cars in the USA*. Cambridge: Cambridge University Press.

Standard and Poor's. 1981a. *Industry Surveys Auto-Auto Parts, Basic Analysis*. New York: Standard and Poor's, Inc. Also 1975 and 1979 issues.

_____. 1981b. Stock Report. New York: Standard and Poor's, Inc.

Sweeney, James L. 1979. *Passenger Car Gasoline Demand Model*. Working Paper. Department of Engineering-Economic Systems. Stanford, Calif.: Stanford University. November 1979.

Tardiff, T. J. 1980. "Vehicle Choice Models: Review of Previous Studies and Directions for Further Research." *Transportation Research*. New York: Pergamon Press. October-December 1980.

Tucker, William. 1980. "The Wreck of the Auto Industry." *Harper's.* November 1980, pp. 45-60.

Ture, Normal B., and B. Kenneth Sanden. 1977. *The Effects of Tax Policy on Capital Formation.* Financial Executives Research Foundation.

U.S. Bureau of the Census. 1981. *Statistical Abstracts of the United States 1980.* 101 ed. Washington, D.C.

U.S. Congress, House. Committee on Banking, Finance, and Urban Affairs. 1981a. *Findings of the Chrysler Corporation Loan Guarantee Board.* 97th Cong., 1st sess., Committee Print 97-1. Washington, D.C.: Government Printing Office. January 19, 1981.

_____ . 1981b. *To Determine the Impact of Foreign Sourcing on Industry and Communities.* Hearings, 97th Cong., 1st sess., Serial No. 97-12. Washington, D.C.: Government Printing Offices. April 24, 1981.

U.S. Congress, House. Committee on Ways and Means. 1980. *Auto Situation, Autumn 1980.* Hearings, 96th Cong., 2d sess., Serial 96-132. November 18, 1980.

U.S. Congress, Senate. Committee on Commerce, Science and Transportation. 1981. *Government Regulations Affecting the U.S. Automobile Industry.* Hearings, 97th Cong., 1st sess., Serial No. 97-4. January 28, 1981.

U.S. Department of Energy. 1981. *1981 Annual Report to Congress, Volume Three: Forecasts.* Energy Information Administration. Washington, D.C.: Government Printing Office.

U.S. Department of Labor. 1981a. "Estimated Hourly Compensation of Production Workers in the Motor Vehicles and Equipment Industries, Fourteen Countries, 1975-1980." Unpublished data prepared by Bureau of Labor Statistics, Office of Productivity and Technology. March 1981.

_____ . 1981b. "Estimated Hourly Compensation of Production Workers in Manufacturing, Thirty-Three Countries, 1975-1980." Unpublished data prepared by Bureau of Labor Statistics, Office of Productivity and Technology. March 1981.

_____ . 1979. *Handbook of Labor Statistics 1978.* Bureau of Labor Statistics. Washington, D.C.: Government Printing Office.

_____ . 1978. *Handbook of Labor Statistics 1977.* Bureau of Labor Statistics. Washington, D.C.: Government Printing Office.

U.S. Department of Transportation. 1981a. *The U.S. Automobile Industry, 1980 – Report to the President from the Secretary of Transportation.* Office of the Secretary of Transportation, Office of the Assistant Secretary for Policy and International Affairs and Transportation Systems Center. DOT-P-10-81-02. January 1981.

_____ . 1981b. "Federal Motor Vehicle Safety Standards and Procedures." National Highway Traffic Safety Administration. DOT HS 805 674.

_____ . 1980. *Automobile Occupant Crash Protection-Progress Report No. 3.* National Highway Traffic Safety Administration. July 1980.

_____ . 1979a. *Contributions of Automobile Regulation.* National Highway Traffic Safety Administration. DOT/HS-805-501. December 1979.

_____ . 1979b. *Fatal Accident Reporting System.* National Highway Traffic Safety Administration. Washington, D.C.: Government Printing Office.

_____ . 1978. *Alcohol and Highway Safety: A Review of the State of Knowledge-Summary Volume.* National Highway Traffic Safety Administration. Washington, D.C.: Government Printing Office. This is based on work by Ralph K. Jones and Kent B. Joscelyn of the University of Michigan.

_____ . Issues 1971-81. *Safety Related Recall Campaigns for Motor Vehicles and Motor Vehicle Equipment, Including Tires.* (Called *Motor Vehicle Safety Defect Recall Campaigns* prior to 1976.) National Highway Traffic Safety Administration. Washington, D.C.: Government Printing Office.

U.S. International Trade Commission. 1980. *Certain Motor Vehicles and Certain Chassis and Bodies Therefor.* USITC Publication 110. Washington, D.C. December 1980.

Value Line. 1981. Investment Reports. New York.

Wards Automotive News. 1976. Detroit: Wards Communication Corporation.

Washington Post. 1981. "A Search for Quality: Detroit Tries It All." August 23, 1981.

White House. 1981. *Actions to Help the U.S. Auto Industry.* Office of the Press Secretary. April 6, 1981.

White, Lawrence J. 1976. "American Automotive Emissions Control Policy — A Review of the Reviews." *Journal of Environmental Economics and Management*. April 1976, pp. 231-246.

_____ . 1975. "Proposal for Restructuring the Automobile Industry." *Antitrust Law and Economics Review*. vol. 7, no. 3, pp. 69-102.

_____ . 1971. *The Automobile Industry Since 1945*. Cambridge, Mass.: Harvard University Press.

Wykoff, F. C. 1973. "User Cost Approach to New Automobile Purchases." *The Review of Economic Studies*. vol. 40, no. 123, pp. 377-390.

Index

About the Authors

N. P. Kannan is a Vice President of Ganesa Group International Incorporated, a Virginia-based firm specializing in customized mini- and microcomputer software. Prior to this position, he was an independent consultant in economics, finance, and strategic planning. Kannan was also previously associated with the MITRE Corporation as a senior economist. He is the author of several papers and a book entitled *Energy, Economic Growth, and Equity in the United States* (Praeger, 1979).

Kathy K. Rebibo received her training in mathematics at the University of Illinois, the University of Maryland, and the University of Heidelberg. She is presently a Senior Systems Scientist at the MITRE Corporation specializing in computer simulation and applied mathematics and a consultant for NASA in the design of local area networks. Rebibo has authored several reports and papers, the most recent of which is entitled "Fuel Efficiency and the U.S. Auto Industry," with N. P. Kannan and Donna L. Ellis.

Donna L. Ellis is an Economist and Cost Analyst with the MITRE Corporation. For the past two years she has contributed to the MITRE automobile industry project and cost analysis for the U.S. Navy communications systems. She has also participated in numerous projects for the National Science Foundation, the U.S. Department of Energy, and the U.S. Department of Housing and Urban development. She received her training in economics at the George Mason University.